Artificial Intelligence with Python

AI With Python - A Beginner's Guide

AI With Python Tutorial for Beginners

Artificial intelligence (AI) is the simulation of human intelligence processes by machines, especially computer systems. These processes include learning (the acquisition of information and rules for using the information), reasoning (using rules to reach approximate or definite conclusions) and self-correction. Particular applications of AI include expert systems, speech recognition and machine vision.

Artificial Intelligence is the ability of machines to seemingly think for themselves. AI is demonstrated when a task, formerly performed by a human and thought of as requiring the ability to learn, reason and solve problems, can now be done by a machine. A prime example is an autonomous vehicle. The vehicle is able to perceive its surroundings and make decisions in order to safely reach its destination with no human intervention. Converging technologies along with Big Data and the Internet of Things (IoT) are driving the growth of AI. Machines communicate with one another and are now capable of advanced perception, capturing millions of data points in seconds, processing the information and making decisions, all in a matter of seconds. As AI evolves, machines will have more capability to physically act based on their intelligence, eventually leading to machines that can build better versions of themselves.

This tutorial covers the basic concepts of various fields of artificial intelligence like Artificial Neural Networks, Natural Language Processing, Machine Learning, Deep Learning, Genetic algorithms etc., and its implementation in Python.

To whom this tutorial is designed for:

This tutorial will be useful for graduates, post graduates, and research students who either have an interest in this subject or have this subject as a part of their curriculum. The reader can be a beginner or an advanced learner.

Prerequisites:

We assume that the reader has basic knowledge about Artificial Intelligence and Python programming. Reader should be aware about basic terminologies used in AI along with some useful python packages like nltk, OpenCV, pandas, OpenAI Gym, etc.

Table of Contents

AI with Python – Getting Started 36

AI with Python – Supervised Learning: Classification

AI with Python – Deep Learning 304

AI With Python – Introduction

Since the invention of computers or machines, their capability to perform various tasks has experienced an exponential growth. Humans have developed the power of computer systems in terms of their diverse working domains, their increasing speed, and reducing size with respect to time.

A branch of Computer Science named Artificial Intelligence pursues creating the computers or machines as intelligent as human beings.

Artificial intelligence's progress is staggering. Efforts to advance AI concepts over the past 20 years have resulted in some truly amazing innovations. Big data, medical research, and autonomous vehicles are just some of the incredible applications emerging from AI development.

To understand some of the deeper concepts, such as data mining, natural language processing, and driving software, you need to know the three basic AI concepts: machine learning, deep learning, and neural networks. While AI and machine learning may seem like interchangeable terms, AI is usually considered the broader term, with machine learning and the other two AI concepts a subset of it.

Basic Concept of Artificial Intelligence (AI)

According to the father of Artificial Intelligence, John McCarthy, it is "The science and engineering of making intelligent machines, especially intelligent computer programs".

Artificial Intelligence is a way of making a computer, a computer-controlled robot, or a software think intelligently, in the similar manner the intelligent humans think. AI is accomplished by studying how human brain thinks and how humans learn, decide, and work while trying to solve a problem, and then using the outcomes of this study as a basis of developing intelligent software and systems.

While exploiting the power of the computer systems, the curiosity of human, lead him to wonder, **"Can a machine think and behave like humans do?"**

Thus, the development of AI started with the intention of creating similar intelligence in machines that we find and regard high in humans.

The Necessity of Learning AI:

As we know that AI pursues creating the machines as intelligent as human beings. There are numerous reasons for us to study AI. The reasons are as follows −

AI can learn through data

In our daily life, we deal with huge amount of data and human brain cannot keep track of so much data. That is why we need to automate the things. For doing automation, we need to study AI because it can learn from data and can do the repetitive tasks with accuracy and without tiredness.

AI can teach itself

It is very necessary that a system should teach itself because the data itself keeps changing and the knowledge which is derived from such data must be updated constantly. We can use AI to fulfill this purpose because an AI enabled system can teach itself.

AI can respond in real time

Artificial intelligence with the help of neural networks can analyze the data more deeply. Due to this capability, AI can think and respond to the situations which are based on the conditions in real time.

AI achieves accuracy

With the help of deep neural networks, AI can achieve tremendous accuracy. AI helps in the field of medicine to diagnose diseases such as cancer from the MRIs of patients.

AI can organize data to get most out of it

The data is an intellectual property for the systems which are using self-learning algorithms. We need AI to index and organize the data in a way that it always gives the best results.

Understanding Intelligence:

With AI, smart systems can be built. We need to understand the concept of intelligence so that our brain can construct another intelligence system like itself.

What is Intelligence?

The ability of a system to calculate, reason, perceive relationships and analogies, learn from experience, store and retrieve information from memory, solve problems, comprehend complex ideas, use natural language fluently, classify, generalize, and adapt new situations.

Types of Intelligence

As described by Howard Gardner, an American developmental psychologist, Intelligence comes in multifold −

Sr.No	Intelligence & Description	Example
1	**Linguistic intelligence** The ability to speak, recognize, and use mechanisms of phonology (speech sounds), syntax (grammar), and semantics (meaning).	Narrators, Orators
2	**Musical intelligence** The ability to create, communicate with, and understand meanings made of sound, understanding of pitch, rhythm.	Musicians, Singers, Composers
3	**Logical-mathematical**	Mathematicians,

	intelligence The ability to use and understand relationships in the absence of action or objects. It is also the ability to understand complex and abstract ideas.	Scientists
4	**Spatial intelligence** The ability to perceive visual or spatial information, change it, and re-create visual images without reference to the objects, construct 3D images, and to move and rotate them.	Map readers, Astronauts, Physicists
5	**Bodily-Kinesthetic intelligence** The ability to use complete or part of the body to solve problems or fashion products, control over fine and coarse motor skills, and manipulate the objects.	Players, Dancers

6	**Intra-personal intelligence**	
	The ability to distinguish among one's own feelings, intentions, and motivations.	Gautam Buddhha
7	**Interpersonal intelligence**	
	The ability to recognize and make distinctions among other people's feelings, beliefs, and intentions.	Mass Communicators, Interviewers

You can say a machine or a system is artificially intelligent when it is equipped with at least one or all intelligences in it.

What is Intelligence Composed Of?

The intelligence is intangible. It is composed of −

- Reasoning
- Learning
- Problem Solving
- Perception
- Linguistic Intelligence

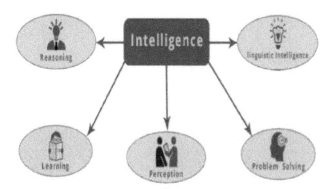

Let us go through all the components briefly —

Reasoning

It is the set of processes that enable us to provide basis for judgement, making decisions, and prediction. There are broadly two types —

Inductive Reasoning	Deductive Reasoning
It conducts specific observations to makes broad general statements.	It starts with a general statement and examines the possibilities to reach a specific,

	logical conclusion.
Even if all of the premises are true in a statement, inductive reasoning allows for the conclusion to be false.	If something is true of a class of things in general, it is also true for all members of that class.
Example – "Nita is a teacher. Nita is studious. Therefore, All teachers are studious."	**Example** – "All women of age above 60 years are grandmothers. Shalini is 65 years. Therefore, Shalini is a grandmother."

Learning – 1

The ability of learning is possessed by humans, particular species of animals, and AI-enabled systems. Learning is categorized as follows –

Auditory Learning

It is learning by listening and hearing. For example, students listening to recorded audio lectures.

Episodic Learning

To learn by remembering sequences of events that one has witnessed or experienced. This is linear and orderly.

Motor Learning

It is learning by precise movement of muscles. For example, picking objects, writing, etc.

Observational Learning

To learn by watching and imitating others. For example, child tries to learn by mimicking her parent.

Perceptual Learning

It is learning to recognize stimuli that one has seen before. For example, identifying and classifying objects and situations.

Relational Learning:

It involves learning to differentiate among various stimuli on the basis of relational properties, rather than absolute properties. For Example, Adding 'little less' salt at the time of cooking potatoes that came up salty last time, when cooked with adding say a tablespoon of salt.

- **Spatial Learning** – It is learning through visual stimuli such as images, colors, maps, etc. For example, A person can create roadmap in mind before actually following the road.

- **Stimulus-Response Learning** – It is learning to perform a particular behavior when a certain stimulus is present. For example, a dog raises its ear on hearing doorbell.

Problem Solving:

It is the process in which one perceives and tries to arrive at a desired solution from a present situation by taking some path, which is blocked by known or unknown hurdles.

Problem solving also includes **decision making**, which is the process of selecting the best suitable alternative out of multiple alternatives to reach the desired goal.

Perception:

It is the process of acquiring, interpreting, selecting, and organizing sensory information.

Perception presumes **sensing**. In humans, perception is aided by sensory organs. In the domain of AI, perception mechanism puts the data acquired by the sensors together in a meaningful manner.

Linguistic Intelligence:

It is one's ability to use, comprehend, speak, and write the verbal and written language. It is important in interpersonal communication.

What's involved in AI:

Artificial intelligence is a vast area of study. This field of study helps in finding solutions to real world problems.

Let us now see the different fields of study within AI −

Machine Learning

It is one of the most popular fields of AI. The basic concept of this filed is to make the machine learning from data as the human beings can learn from his/her experience. It contains learning models on the basis of which the predictions can be made on unknown data.

Logic

It is another important field of study in which mathematical logic is used to execute the computer programs. It contains rules and facts to perform pattern matching, semantic analysis, etc.

Searching

This field of study is basically used in games like chess, tic-tac-toe. Search algorithms give the optimal solution after searching the whole search space.

Artificial Neural Networks

This is a network of efficient computing systems the central theme of which is borrowed from the analogy of biological neural networks. ANN can be used in robotics, speech recognition, speech processing, etc.

Genetic Algorithm

Genetic algorithms help in solving problems with the assistance of more than one program. The result would be based on selecting the fittest.

Knowledge Representation

It is the field of study with the help of which we can represent the facts in a way the machine that is understandable to the machine. The more efficiently knowledge is represented; the more system would be intelligent.

Application of AI:

In this section, we will see the different fields supported by AI –

Gaming

AI plays crucial role in strategic games such as chess, poker, tic-tac-toe, etc., where machine can think of large number of possible positions based on heuristic knowledge.

Natural Language Processing

It is possible to interact with the computer that understands natural language spoken by humans.

Expert Systems

There are some applications which integrate machine, software, and special information to impart reasoning and advising. They provide explanation and advice to the users.

Vision Systems

These systems understand, interpret, and comprehend visual input on the computer. For example,

- A spying aeroplane takes photographs, which are used to figure out spatial information or map of the areas.

- Doctors use clinical expert system to diagnose the patient.

- Police use computer software that can recognize the face of criminal with the stored portrait made by forensic artist.

Speech Recognition

Some intelligent systems are capable of hearing and comprehending the language in terms of sentences and their meanings while a human talks to it. It can handle different accents, slang words, noise in the background, change in human's noise due to cold, etc.

Handwriting Recognition

The handwriting recognition software reads the text written on paper by a pen or on screen by a stylus. It can recognize the shapes of the letters and convert it into editable text.

Intelligent Robots

Robots are able to perform the tasks given by a human. They have sensors to detect physical data from the real world such as light, heat, temperature, movement, sound, bump, and pressure. They have efficient processors, multiple sensors and huge memory, to exhibit intelligence. In addition, they are capable of learning from their mistakes and they can adapt to the new environment.

Cognitive Modeling: Simulating Human Thinking Procedure

Cognitive modeling is basically the field of study within computer science that deals with the study and simulating the thinking process of human beings. The main task of AI is to make machine think like human. The most important feature of human thinking process is problem solving. That is why more or less cognitive modeling tries to understand how humans can solve the problems. After that this model can be used for various AI applications such as machine learning, robotics, natural language processing, etc. Following is the diagram of different thinking levels of human brain −

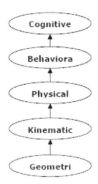

Agent & Environment:

In this section, we will focus on the agent and environment and how these help in Artificial Intelligence.

Agent

An agent is anything that can perceive its environment through sensors and acts upon that environment through effectors.

- A **human agent** has sensory organs such as eyes, ears, nose, tongue and skin parallel to the sensors, and other organs such as hands, legs, mouth, for effectors.

- A **robotic agent** replaces cameras and infrared range finders for the sensors, and various motors and actuators for effectors.

- A **software agent** has encoded bit strings as its programs and actions.

Environment:

Some programs operate in an entirely **artificial environment**confined to keyboard input, database, computer file systems and character output on a screen.

In contrast, some software agents (software robots or softbots) exist in rich, unlimited softbots domains. The simulator has a **very detailed, complex environment**. The software agent needs to choose from a long array of actions in real time. A softbot is designed to scan the online preferences of the customer and shows interesting items to the customer works in the **real** as well as an **artificial** environment.

AI with Python – Getting Started

In this chapter, we will learn how to get started with Python. We will also understand how Python helps for Artificial Intelligence.

Why Python for AI?

Artificial intelligence is considered to be the trending technology of the future. Already there are a number of applications made on it. Due to this, many companies and researchers are taking interest in it. But the main question that arises here is that in which programming language can these AI applications be developed? There are various programming languages like Lisp, Prolog, C++, Java and Python, which can be used for developing applications of AI. Among them, Python programming language gains a huge popularity and the reasons are as follows –

Simple syntax & less coding

Python involves very less coding and simple syntax among other programming languages which can be used for developing AI applications. Due to this feature, the testing can be easier and we can focus more on programming.

Inbuilt libraries for AI projects

A major advantage for using Python for AI is that it comes with inbuilt libraries. Python has libraries for almost all kinds of AI projects. For example, **NumPy, SciPy, matplotlib, nltk, SimpleAI** are some the important inbuilt libraries of Python.

- **Open source** – Python is an open source programming language. This makes it widely popular in the community.

- **Can be used for broad range of programming** – Python can be used for a broad range of programming tasks like small shell script to enterprise web applications. This is another reason Python is suitable for AI projects.

Features of Python:

Python is a high-level, interpreted, interactive and object-oriented scripting language. Python is designed to be highly readable. It uses English keywords frequently where as other languages use punctuation, and it has fewer syntactical constructions than other languages. Python's features include the following −

- **Easy-to-learn** − Python has few keywords, simple structure, and a clearly defined syntax. This allows the student to pick up the language quickly.

- **Easy-to-read** − Python code is more clearly defined and visible to the eyes.

- **Easy-to-maintain** − Python's source code is fairly easy-to-maintain.

- **A broad standard library** − Python's bulk of the library is very portable and cross-platform compatible on UNIX, Windows, and Macintosh.

- **Interactive Mode** − Python has support for an interactive mode which allows interactive testing and debugging of snippets of code.

- **Portable** − Python can run on a wide variety of hardware platforms and has the same interface on all platforms.

- **Extendable** – We can add low-level modules to the Python interpreter. These modules enable programmers to add to or customize their tools to be more efficient.

- **Databases** – Python provides interfaces to all major commercial databases.

- **GUI Programming** – Python supports GUI applications that can be created and ported to many system calls, libraries and windows systems, such as Windows MFC, Macintosh, and the X Window system of Unix.

- **Scalable** – Python provides a better structure and support for large programs than shell scripting.

Important features of Python:

Let us now consider the following important features of Python –

- It supports functional and structured programming methods as well as OOP.

- It can be used as a scripting language or can be compiled to byte-code for building large applications.

- It provides very high-level dynamic data types and supports dynamic type checking.

- It supports automatic garbage collection.

- It can be easily integrated with C, C++, COM, ActiveX, CORBA, and Java.

Installing Python:

Python distribution is available for a large number of platforms. You need to download only the binary code applicable for your platform and install Python.

If the binary code for your platform is not available, you need a C compiler to compile the source code manually. Compiling the source code offers more flexibility in terms of choice of features that you require in your installation.

Here is a quick overview of installing Python on various platforms −

Unix and Linux Installation:

Follow these steps to install Python on Unix/Linux machine.

- Open a Web browser and go to https://www.python.org/downloads

- Follow the link to download zipped source code available for Unix/Linux.

- Download and extract files.

- Editing the *Modules/Setup* file if you want to customize some options.

- run ./configure script

- make

- make install

This installs Python at the standard location /usr/local/bin and its libraries at */usr/local/lib/pythonXX* where XX is the version of Python.

Windows Installation:

Follow these steps to install Python on Windows machine.

- Open a Web browser and go to https://www.python.org/downloads

- Follow the link for the Windows installer *python-XYZ*.msi file where XYZ is the version you need to install.

- To use this installer *python-XYZ*.msi, the Windows system must support Microsoft Installer 2.0. Save the installer file to your local machine and then run it to find out if your machine supports MSI.

- Run the downloaded file. This brings up the Python install wizard, which is really easy to use. Just accept the default settings and wait until the install is finished.

Macintosh Installation:

If you are on Mac OS X, it is recommended that you use Homebrew to install Python 3. It is a great package installer for Mac OS X and it is really easy to use. If you don't have Homebrew, you can install it using the following command −

```
$ ruby -e "$(curl -fsSL
https://raw.githubusercontent.com/Homebrew/install/master/install)"
```

We can update the package manager with the command below −

```
$ brew update
```

Now run the following command to install Python3 on your system −

```
$ brew install python3
```

Setting up PATH:

Programs and other executable files can be in many directories, so operating systems provide a search path that lists the directories that the OS searches for executables.

The path is stored in an environment variable, which is a named string maintained by the operating system. This variable contains information available to the command shell and other programs.

The path variable is named as PATH in Unix or Path in Windows (Unix is case-sensitive; Windows is not).

In Mac OS, the installer handles the path details. To invoke the Python interpreter from any particular directory, you must add the Python directory to your path.

Setting Path at Unix/Linux:

To add the Python directory to the path for a particular session in Unix –

- In the csh shell

Type **setenv PATH "$PATH:/usr/local/bin/python"**

and press **Enter**.

- In the bash shell (Linux)

Type **export ATH = "$PATH:/usr/local/bin/python"**

and press **Enter**.

- In the sh or ksh shell

Type **PATH ="$PATH:/usr/local/bin/python"**

and press **Enter**.

Note – /usr/local/bin/python is the path of the Python directory.

Setting Path at Windows:

To add the Python directory to the path for a particular session in Windows −

- **At the command prompt** − type **path %path%;C:\Python** and press **Enter.**

Note − C:\Python is the path of the Python directory.

Running Python:

Let us now see the different ways to run Python. The ways are described below −

Interactive Interpreter

We can start Python from Unix, DOS, or any other system that provides you a command-line interpreter or shell window.

- Enter **python** at the command line.

- Start coding right away in the interactive interpreter.

$python # Unix/Linux

or

python% # Unix/Linux

or

C:> python # Windows/DOS

Here is the list of all the available command line options −

S.No.	Option & Description
1	**-d** It provides debug output.
2	**-o** It generates optimized bytecode (resulting in .pyo files).
3	**-S** Do not run import site to look for Python paths on startup.
4	**-v** Verbose output (detailed trace on import statements).
5	**-x** Disables class-based built-in exceptions (just use strings); obsolete starting with version 1.6.

6	**-c cmd**
	Runs Python script sent in as cmd string.
7	**File**
	Run Python script from given file.

Script from the Command-line

A Python script can be executed at the command line by invoking the interpreter on your application, as in the following −

$python script.py # Unix/Linux

or,

python% script.py # Unix/Linux

or,

C:> python script.py # Windows/DOS

Note − Be sure the file permission mode allows execution.

Integrated Development Environment

You can run Python from a Graphical User Interface (GUI) environment as well, if you have a GUI application on your system that supports Python.

- **Unix** − IDLE is the very first Unix IDE for Python.

- **Windows** − PythonWin is the first Windows interface for Python and is an IDE with a GUI.

- **Macintosh** − The Macintosh version of Python along with the IDLE IDE is available from the main website, downloadable as either MacBinary or BinHex'd files.

If you are not able to set up the environment properly, then you can take help from your system admin. Make sure the Python environment is properly set up and working perfectly fine.

We can also use another Python platform called Anaconda. It includes hundreds of popular data science packages and the conda package and virtual environment manager for Windows, Linux and MacOS. You can download it as per your operating system from the link https://www.anaconda.com/download/.

AI with Python – Machine Learning

Learning means the acquisition of knowledge or skills through study or experience. Based on this, we can define machine learning (ML) as follows −

It may be defined as the field of computer science, more specifically an application of artificial intelligence, which provides computer systems the ability to learn with data and improve from experience without being explicitly programmed.

Basically, the main focus of machine learning is to allow the computers learn automatically without human intervention. Now the question arises that how such learning can be started and done? It can be started with the observations of data. The data can be some examples, instruction or some direct experiences too. Then on the basis of this input, machine makes better decision by looking for some patterns in data.

Types of Machine Learning (ML)

Machine Learning Algorithms helps computer system learn without being explicitly programmed. These algorithms are categorized into supervised or unsupervised. Let us now see a few algorithms −

Supervised machine learning algorithms

This is the most commonly used machine learning algorithm. It is called supervised because the process of algorithm learning from the training dataset can be thought of as a teacher supervising the learning process. In this kind of ML algorithm, the possible outcomes are already known and training data is also labeled with correct answers. It can be understood as follows −

Suppose we have input variables **x** and an output variable **y** and we applied an algorithm to learn the mapping function from the input to output such as −

$Y = f(x)$

Now, the main goal is to approximate the mapping function so well that when we have new input data (x), we can predict the output variable (Y) for that data.

Mainly supervised leaning problems can be divided into the following two kinds of problems −

- **Classification** − A problem is called classification problem when we have the categorized output such as "black", "teaching", "non-teaching", etc.

- **Regression** − A problem is called regression problem when we have the real value output such as "distance", "kilogram", etc.

Decision tree, random forest, knn, logistic regression are the examples of supervised machine learning algorithms.

Unsupervised machine learning algorithms

As the name suggests, these kinds of machine learning algorithms do not have any supervisor to provide any sort of guidance. That is why unsupervised machine learning algorithms are closely aligned with what some call true artificial intelligence. It can be understood as follows −

Suppose we have input variable x, then there will be no corresponding output variables as there is in supervised learning algorithms.

In simple words, we can say that in unsupervised learning there will be no correct answer and no teacher for the guidance. Algorithms help to discover interesting patterns in data.

Unsupervised learning problems can be divided into the following two kinds of problem −

- **Clustering** − In clustering problems, we need to discover the inherent groupings in the data. For example, grouping customers by their purchasing behavior.

- **Association** − A problem is called association problem because such kinds of problem require discovering the rules that describe large portions of our data. For example, finding the customers who buy both **x** and **y**.

K-means for clustering, Apriori algorithm for association are the examples of unsupervised machine learning algorithms.

Reinforcement machine learning algorithms

These kinds of machine learning algorithms are used very less. These algorithms train the systems to make specific decisions. Basically, the machine is exposed to an environment where it trains itself continually using the trial and error method. These algorithms learn from past experience and tries to capture the best possible knowledge to make accurate decisions. Markov Decision Process is an example of reinforcement machine learning algorithms.

Most Common Machine Learning Algorithms

In this section, we will learn about the most common machine learning algorithms. The algorithms are described below −

Linear Regression

It is one of the most well-known algorithms in statistics and machine learning.

Basic concept − Mainly linear regression is a linear model that assumes a linear relationship between the input variables say x and the single output variable say y. In other words, we can say that y can be calculated from a linear combination of the input variables x. The relationship between variables can be established by fitting a best line.

Types of Linear Regression

Linear regression is of the following two types −

- **Simple linear regression** − A linear regression algorithm is called simple linear regression if it is having only one independent variable.

- **Multiple linear regression** − A linear regression algorithm is called multiple linear regression if it is having more than one independent variable.

Linear regression is mainly used to estimate the real values based on continuous variable(s). For example, the total sale of a shop in a day, based on real values, can be estimated by linear regression.

Logistic Regression

It is a classification algorithm and also known as **logit**regression.

Mainly logistic regression is a classification algorithm that is used to estimate the discrete values like 0 or 1, true or false, yes or no based on a given set of independent variable. Basically, it predicts the probability hence its output lies in between 0 and 1.

Decision Tree

Decision tree is a supervised learning algorithm that is mostly used for classification problems.

Basically it is a classifier expressed as recursive partition based on the independent variables. Decision tree has nodes which form the rooted tree. Rooted tree is a directed tree with a node called "root". Root does not have any incoming edges and all the other nodes have one incoming edge. These nodes are called leaves or decision nodes. For example, consider the following decision tree to see whether a person is fit or not.

Support Vector Machine (SVM)

It is used for both classification and regression problems. But mainly it is used for classification problems. The main concept of SVM is to plot each data item as a point in n-dimensional space with the value of each feature being the value of a particular coordinate. Here n would be the features we would have. Following is a simple graphical representation to understand the concept of SVM −

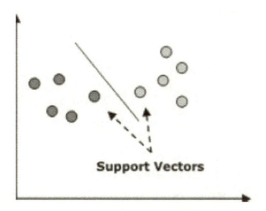

Support Vectors

In the above diagram, we have two features hence we first need to plot these two variables in two dimensional space where each point has two co-ordinates, called support vectors. The line splits the data into two different classified groups. This line would be the classifier.

Naïve Bayes

It is also a classification technique. The logic behind this classification technique is to use Bayes theorem for building classifiers. The assumption is that the predictors are independent. In simple words, it assumes that the presence of a particular feature in a class is unrelated to the presence of any other feature. Below is the equation for Bayes theorem −

$P(AB)=P(BA)P(A)P(B)P(AB)=P(BA)P(A)P(B)$

The Naïve Bayes model is easy to build and particularly useful for large data sets.

K-Nearest Neighbors (KNN)

It is used for both classification and regression of the problems. It is widely used to solve classification problems. The main concept of this algorithm is that it used to store all the available cases and classifies new cases by majority votes of its k neighbors. The case being then assigned to the class which is the most common amongst its K-nearest neighbors, measured by a distance function. The distance function can be Euclidean, Minkowski and Hamming distance. Consider the following to use KNN −

- Computationally KNN are expensive than other algorithms used for classification problems.

- The normalization of variables needed otherwise higher range variables can bias it.

- In KNN, we need to work on pre-processing stage like noise removal.

K-Means Clustering

As the name suggests, it is used to solve the clustering problems. It is basically a type of unsupervised learning. The main logic of K-Means clustering algorithm is to classify the data set through a number of clusters. Follow these steps to form clusters by K-means −

- K-means picks k number of points for each cluster known as centroids.

- Now each data point forms a cluster with the closest centroids, i.e., k clusters.

- Now, it will find the centroids of each cluster based on the existing cluster members.

- We need to repeat these steps until convergence occurs.

Random Forest

It is a supervised classification algorithm. The advantage of random forest algorithm is that it can be used for both classification and regression kind of problems. Basically it is the collection of decision trees (i.e., forest) or you can say ensemble of the decision trees. The basic concept of random forest is that each tree gives a classification and the forest chooses the best classifications from them.

Followings are the advantages of Random Forest algorithm −

- Random forest classifier can be used for both classification and regression tasks.

- They can handle the missing values.

- It won't over fit the model even if we have more number of trees in the forest.

AI with Python – Data Preparation

We have already studied supervised as well as unsupervised machine learning algorithms. These algorithms require formatted data to start the training process. We must prepare or format data in a certain way so that it can be supplied as an input to ML algorithms.

This chapter focuses on data preparation for machine learning algorithms.

Preprocessing the Data

In our daily life, we deal with lots of data but this data is in raw form. To provide the data as the input of machine learning algorithms, we need to convert it into a meaningful data. That is where data preprocessing comes into picture. In other simple words, we can say that before providing the data to the machine learning algorithms we need to preprocess the data.

Data preprocessing steps

Follow these steps to preprocess the data in Python −

Step 1 − Importing the useful packages − If we are using Python then this would be the first step for converting the data into a certain format, i.e., preprocessing. It can be done as follows −

```
import numpy as np
import sklearn.preprocessing
```

Here we have used the following two packages –

- **NumPy** – Basically NumPy is a general purpose array-processing package designed to efficiently manipulate large multi-dimensional arrays of arbitrary records without sacrificing too much speed for small multi-dimensional arrays.

- **Sklearn.preprocessing** – This package provides many common utility functions and transformer classes to change raw feature vectors into a representation that is more suitable for machine learning algorithms.

Step 2 – Defining sample data – After importing the packages, we need to define some sample data so that we can apply preprocessing techniques on that data. We will now define the following sample data –

```
Input_data = np.array([2.1, -1.9, 5.5],

            [-1.5, 2.4, 3.5],

            [0.5, -7.9, 5.6],

            [5.9, 2.3, -5.8])
```

Step3 – Applying preprocessing technique – In this step, we need to apply any of the preprocessing techniques.

The following section describes the data preprocessing techniques.

Techniques for Data Preprocessing

The techniques for data preprocessing are described below –

Binarization

This is the preprocessing technique which is used when we need to convert our numerical values into Boolean values. We can use an inbuilt method to binarize the input data say by using 0.5 as the threshold value in the following way –

```
data_binarized = preprocessing.Binarizer(threshold = 0.5).transform(input_data)

print("\nBinarized data:\n", data_binarized)
```

Now, after running the above code we will get the following output, all the values above 0.5(threshold value) would be converted to 1 and all the values below 0.5 would be converted to 0.

Binarized data

```
[[ 1. 0. 1.]
 [ 0. 1. 1.]
 [ 0. 0. 1.]
 [ 1. 1. 0.]]
```

Mean Removal

It is another very common preprocessing technique that is used in machine learning. Basically it is used to eliminate the mean from feature vector so that every feature is centered on zero. We can also remove the bias from the features in the feature vector. For applying mean removal preprocessing technique on the sample data, we can write the Python code shown below. The code will display the Mean and Standard deviation of the input data −

```
print("Mean = ", input_data.mean(axis = 0))
print("Std deviation = ", input_data.std(axis = 0))
```

We will get the following output after running the above lines of code −

```
      Mean = [ 1.75     -1.275     2.2]
Std deviation = [ 2.71431391  4.20022321  4.69414529]
```

Now, the code below will remove the Mean and Standard deviation of the input data −

```
data_scaled = preprocessing.scale(input_data)

print("Mean =", data_scaled.mean(axis=0))

print("Std deviation =", data_scaled.std(axis = 0))
```

We will get the following output after running the above lines of code −

```
    Mean    =    [    1.11022302e-16    0.00000000e+00
0.00000000e+00]
Std deviation = [ 1.        1.        1.]
```

Scaling

It is another data preprocessing technique that is used to scale the feature vectors. Scaling of feature vectors is needed because the values of every feature can vary between many random values. In other words we can say that scaling is important because we do not want any feature to be synthetically large or small. With the help of the following Python code, we can do the scaling of our input data, i.e., feature vector −

 # Min max scaling

```
data_scaler_minmax                                    =
preprocessing.MinMaxScaler(feature_range=(0,1))

data_scaled_minmax                                    =
data_scaler_minmax.fit_transform(input_data)
```

```
print ("\nMin max scaled data:\n", data_scaled_minmax)
```

We will get the following output after running the above lines of code –

Min max scaled data

```
[ [ 0.48648649  0.58252427  0.99122807]
 [ 0.         1.         0.81578947]
 [ 0.27027027 0.         1.        ]
 [ 1.         0. 99029126 0.        ]]
```

Normalization

It is another data preprocessing technique that is used to modify the feature vectors. Such kind of modification is necessary to measure the feature vectors on a common scale. Followings are two types of normalization which can be used in machine learning –

L1 Normalization

It is also referred to as **Least Absolute Deviations**. This kind of normalization modifies the values so that the sum of the absolute values is always up to 1 in each row. It can be implemented on the input data with the help of the following Python code −

```
# Normalize data
data_normalized_l1 = preprocessing.normalize(input_data,
norm = 'l1')
print("\nL1 normalized data:\n", data_normalized_l1)
```

The above line of code generates the following output &miuns;

```
L1 normalized data:
[[ 0.22105263 -0.2        0.57894737]
 [-0.2027027   0.32432432  0.47297297]
 [ 0.03571429 -0.56428571  0.4       ]
 [ 0.42142857  0.16428571 -0.41428571]]
```

L2 Normalization

It is also referred to as **least squares**. This kind of normalization modifies the values so that the sum of the squares is always up to 1 in each row. It can be implemented on the input data with the help of the following Python code −

```
# Normalize data
data_normalized_l2 = preprocessing.normalize(input_data,
norm = 'l2')
print("\nL2 normalized data:\n", data_normalized_l2)
```

The above line of code will generate the following output −

L2 normalized data:
[[0.33946114 -0.30713151 0.88906489]
[-0.33325106 0.53320169 0.7775858]
[0.05156558 -0.81473612 0.57753446]
[0.68706914 0.26784051 -0.6754239]]

Labeling the Data

We already know that data in a certain format is necessary for machine learning algorithms. Another important requirement is that the data must be labelled properly before sending it as the input of machine learning algorithms. For example, if we talk about classification, there are lot of labels on the data. Those labels are in the form of words, numbers, etc. Functions related to machine learning in **sklearn** expect that the data must have number labels. Hence, if the data is in other form then it must be converted to numbers. This process of transforming the word labels into numerical form is called label encoding.

Label encoding steps

Follow these steps for encoding the data labels in Python —

Step1 − Importing the useful packages

If we are using Python then this would be first step for converting the data into certain format, i.e., preprocessing. It can be done as follows −

```
import numpy as np

from sklearn import preprocessing
```

Step 2 – Defining sample labels

After importing the packages, we need to define some sample labels so that we can create and train the label encoder. We will now define the following sample labels –

```
# Sample input labels

input_labels                                    =
['red','black','red','green','black','yellow','white']
```

Step 3 – Creating & training of label encoder object

In this step, we need to create the label encoder and train it. The following Python code will help in doing this –

```
# Creating the label encoder
encoder = preprocessing.LabelEncoder()
encoder.fit(input_labels)
```

Following would be the output after running the above Python code –

```
LabelEncoder()
```

Step4 − Checking the performance by encoding random ordered list

This step can be used to check the performance by encoding the random ordered list. Following Python code can be written to do the same −

```
# encoding a set of labels
test_labels = ['green','red','black']
encoded_values = encoder.transform(test_labels)
print("\nLabels =", test_labels)
```

The labels would get printed as follows −

```
Labels = ['green', 'red', 'black']
```

Now, we can get the list of encoded values i.e. word labels converted to numbers as follows −

```
print("Encoded values =", list(encoded_values))
```

The encoded values would get printed as follows −

```
Encoded values = [1, 2, 0]
```

Step 5 – Checking the performance by decoding a random set of numbers –

This step can be used to check the performance by decoding the random set of numbers. Following Python code can be written to do the same –

```
# decoding a set of values
encoded_values = [3,0,4,1]
decoded_list = encoder.inverse_transform(encoded_values)
print("\nEncoded values =", encoded_values)
```

Now, Encoded values would get printed as follows –

Encoded values = [3, 0, 4, 1]

```
print("\nDecoded labels =", list(decoded_list))
```

Now, decoded values would get printed as follows –

Decoded labels = ['white', 'black', 'yellow', 'green']

Labeled v/s Unlabeled Data

Unlabeled data mainly consists of the samples of natural or human-created object that can easily be obtained from the world. They include, audio, video, photos, news articles, etc.

On the other hand, labeled data takes a set of unlabeled data and augments each piece of that unlabeled data with some tag or label or class that is meaningful. For example, if we have a photo then the label can be put based on the content of the photo, i.e., it is photo of a boy or girl or animal or anything else. Labeling the data needs human expertise or judgment about a given piece of unlabeled data.

There are many scenarios where unlabeled data is plentiful and easily obtained but labeled data often requires a human/expert to annotate. Semi-supervised learning attempts to combine labeled and unlabeled data to build better models.

AI with Python – Supervised Learning: Classification

In this chapter, we will focus on implementing supervised learning – **classification**.

The classification technique or model attempts to get some conclusion from observed values. In classification problem, we have the categorized output such as "Black" or "white" or "Teaching" and "Non-Teaching". While building the classification model, we need to have training dataset that contains data points and the corresponding labels. For example, if we want to check whether the image is of a car or not. For checking this, we will build a training dataset having the two classes related to "car" and "no car". Then we need to train the model by using the training samples. The classification models are mainly used in face recognition, spam identification, etc.

Steps for Building a Classifier in Python

For building a classifier in Python, we are going to use Python 3 and Scikit-learn which is a tool for machine learning. Follow these steps to build a classifier in Python –

Step 1 – Import Scikit-learn

This would be very first step for building a classifier in Python. In this step, we will install a Python package called Scikit-learn which is one of the best machine learning modules in Python. The following command will help us import the package −

```
Import Sklearn
```

Step 2 − Import Scikit-learn's dataset

In this step, we can begin working with the dataset for our machine learning model. Here, we are going to use **the** Breast Cancer Wisconsin Diagnostic Database.

The dataset includes various information about breast cancer tumors, as well as classification labels of **malignant** or **benign**. The dataset has 569 instances, or data, on 569 tumors and includes information on 30 attributes, or features, such as the radius of the tumor, texture, smoothness, and area. With the help of the following command, we can import the Scikit-learn's breast cancer dataset −

```
from sklearn.datasets import load_breast_cancer
```

Now, the following command will load the dataset.

```
data = load_breast_cancer()
```

Following is a list of important dictionary keys −

- Classification label names(target_names)
- The actual labels(target)
- The attribute/feature names(feature_names)

- The attribute (data)

Now, with the help of the following command, we can create new variables for each important set of information and assign the data. In other words, we can organize the data with the following commands —

```
label_names = data['target_names']
labels = data['target']
feature_names = data['feature_names']
features = data['data']
```

Now, to make it clearer we can print the class labels, the first data instance's label, our feature names and the feature's value with the help of the following commands —

```
print(label_names)
```

The above command will print the class names which are malignant and benign respectively. It is shown as the output below —

```
['malignant' 'benign']
```

Now, the command below will show that they are mapped to binary values 0 and 1. Here 0 represents malignant cancer and 1 represents benign cancer. You will receive the following output —

```
print(labels[0])
0
```

The two commands given below will produce the feature names and feature values.

```
print(feature_names[0])
mean radius
print(features[0])
[   1.79900000e+01   1.03800000e+01   1.22800000e+02
1.00100000e+03
   1.18400000e-01   2.77600000e-01   3.00100000e-01
1.47100000e-01
   2.41900000e-01   7.87100000e-02   1.09500000e+00
9.05300000e-01
   8.58900000e+00   1.53400000e+02   6.39900000e-03
4.90400000e-02
   5.37300000e-02   1.58700000e-02   3.00300000e-02
6.19300000e-03
   2.53800000e+01   1.73300000e+01   1.84600000e+02
2.01900000e+03
   1.62200000e-01   6.65600000e-01   7.11900000e-01
2.65400000e-01
   4.60100000e-01 1.18900000e-01]
```

From the above output, we can see that the first data instance is a malignant tumor the radius of which is 1.7990000e+01.

Step 3 – Organizing data into sets

In this step, we will divide our data into two parts namely a training set and a test set. Splitting the data into these sets is very important because we have to test our model on the unseen data. To split the data into sets, sklearn has a function called the **train_test_split()** function. With the help of the following commands, we can split the data in these sets −

```
from sklearn.model_selection import train_test_split
```

The above command will import the **train_test_split** function from sklearn and the command below will split the data into training and test data. In the example given below, we are using 40 % of the data for testing and the remaining data would be used for training the model.

```
train, test, train_labels, test_labels =
train_test_split(features,labels,test_size = 0.40,
random_state = 42)
```

Step 4 − Building the model

In this step, we will be building our model. We are going to use Naïve Bayes algorithm for building the model. Following commands can be used to build the model −

```
from sklearn.naive_bayes import GaussianNB
```

The above command will import the GaussianNB module. Now, the following command will help you initialize the model.

```
gnb = GaussianNB()
```

We will train the model by fitting it to the data by using gnb.fit().

model = gnb.fit(train, train_labels)

Step 5 – Evaluating the model and its accuracy

In this step, we are going to evaluate the model by making predictions on our test data. Then we will find out its accuracy also. For making predictions, we will use the predict() function. The following command will help you do this –

```
preds = gnb.predict(test)
print(preds)
```

```
[1 0 0 1 1 0 0 0 1 1 1 0 1 0 1 0 1 1 1 0 1 1 0 1 1 1 1 1 1
 0 1 1 1 1 1 0 1 0 1 1 0 1 1 1 1 1 1 1 1 0 0 1 1 1 1 1 0
 0 1 1 0 0 1 1 1 0 0 1 1 0 0 1 0 1 1 1 1 1 1 0 1 1 0 0 0 0
 0 1 1 1 1 1 1 1 0 0 1 0 0 1 0 0 1 1 1 0 1 1 0 1 1 0 0 0
 1 1 1 0 0 1 1 0 1 0 0 1 1 0 0 0 1 1 1 0 1 1 0 0 1 0 1 1 0
 1 0 0 1 1 1 1 1 1 1 0 0 1 1 1 1 1 1 1 1 1 1 1 0 1 1 1 0
 1 1 0 1 1 1 1 1 0 0 0 1 1 0 1 0 1 1 1 1 0 1 1 0 1 1 1 0
 1 0 0 1 1 1 1 1 1 1 1 0 1 1 1 1 1 0 1 0 0 1 1 0 1]
```

The above series of 0s and 1s are the predicted values for the tumor classes – malignant and benign.

Now, by comparing the two arrays namely **test_labels** and **preds**, we can find out the accuracy of our model. We are going to use the **accuracy_score()** function to determine the accuracy. Consider the following command for this −

```
from sklearn.metrics import accuracy_score
print(accuracy_score(test_labels,preds))
0.951754385965
```

The result shows that the NaïveBayes classifier is 95.17% accurate.

In this way, with the help of the above steps we can build our classifier in Python.

Building Classifier in Python:

In this section, we will learn how to build a classifier in Python.

Naïve Bayes Classifier

Naïve Bayes is a classification technique used to build classifier using the Bayes theorem. The assumption is that the predictors are independent. In simple words, it assumes that the presence of a particular feature in a class is unrelated to the presence of any other feature. For building Naïve Bayes classifier we need to use the python library called scikit learn. There are three types of Naïve Bayes models named **Gaussian, Multinomial and Bernoulli** under scikit learn package.

To build a Naïve Bayes machine learning classifier model, we need the following &minus

Dataset

We are going to use the dataset named Breast Cancer Wisconsin Diagnostic Database.

The dataset includes various information about breast cancer tumors, as well as classification labels of **malignant** or **benign**. The dataset has 569 instances, or data, on 569 tumors and includes information on 30 attributes, or features, such as the radius of the tumor, texture, smoothness, and area. We can import this dataset from sklearn package.

Naïve Bayes Model

For building Naïve Bayes classifier, we need a Naïve Bayes model. As told earlier, there are three types of Naïve Bayes models named **Gaussian, Multinomial** and **Bernoulli** under scikit learn package. Here, in the following example we are going to use the Gaussian Naïve Bayes model.

By using the above, we are going to build a Naïve Bayes machine learning model to use the tumor information to predict whether or not a tumor is malignant or benign.

To begin with, we need to install the sklearn module. It can be done with the help of the following command −

```
Import Sklearn
```

Now, we need to import the dataset named Breast Cancer Wisconsin Diagnostic Database.

```
from sklearn.datasets import load_breast_cancer
```

Now, the following command will load the dataset.

```
data = load_breast_cancer()
```

The data can be organized as follows −

```
label_names = data['target_names']

labels = data['target']

feature_names = data['feature_names']

features = data['data']
```

Now, to make it clearer we can print the class labels, the first data instance's label, our feature names and the feature's value with the help of following commands −

```
print(label_names)
```

The above command will print the class names which are malignant and benign respectively. It is shown as the output below −

```
['malignant' 'benign']
```

Now, the command given below will show that they are mapped to binary values 0 and 1. Here 0 represents malignant cancer and 1 represents benign cancer. It is shown as the output below −

```
print(labels[0])
0
```

The following two commands will produce the feature names and feature values.

```
print(feature_names[0])
mean radius
print(features[0])
```

```
[  1.79900000e+01    1.03800000e+01    1.22800000e+02
1.00100000e+03
   1.18400000e-01    2.77600000e-01    3.00100000e-01
1.47100000e-01
   2.41900000e-01    7.87100000e-02    1.09500000e+00
9.05300000e-01
   8.58900000e+00    1.53400000e+02    6.39900000e-03
4.90400000e-02
   5.37300000e-02    1.58700000e-02    3.00300000e-02
6.19300000e-03
   2.53800000e+01    1.73300000e+01    1.84600000e+02
2.01900000e+03
   1.62200000e-01    6.65600000e-01    7.11900000e-01
2.65400000e-01
   4.60100000e-01 1.18900000e-01]
```

From the above output, we can see that the first data instance is a malignant tumor the main radius of which is 1.7990000e+01.

For testing our model on unseen data, we need to split our data into training and testing data. It can be done with the help of the following code −

```
from sklearn.model_selection import train_test_split
```

The above command will import the **train_test_split** function from sklearn and the command below will split the data into training and test data. In the below example, we are using 40 % of the data for testing and the remining data would be used for training the model.

```
train, test, train_labels, test_labels =

train_test_split(features,labels,test_size        =        0.40,
random_state = 42)
```

Now, we are building the model with the following commands −

```
from sklearn.naive_bayes import GaussianNB
```

The above command will import the **GaussianNB** module. Now, with the command given below, we need to initialize the model.

```
gnb = GaussianNB()
```

We will train the model by fitting it to the data by using **gnb.fit()**.

```
model = gnb.fit(train, train_labels)
```

Now, evaluate the model by making prediction on the test data and it can be done as follows −

```
preds = gnb.predict(test)
print(preds)
```

[1 0 0 1 1 0 0 0 1 1 1 0 1 0 1 0 1 1 1 0 1 1 0 1 1 1 1 1 1

0 1 1 1 1 1 0 1 0 1 1 0 1 1 1 1 1 1 1 0 0 1 1 1 1 1 0

0 1 1 0 0 1 1 1 0 0 1 1 0 0 1 0 1 1 1 1 1 1 0 1 1 0 0 0 0

0 1 1 1 1 1 1 1 0 0 1 0 0 1 0 0 1 1 1 0 1 1 0 1 1 0 0 0

1 1 1 0 0 1 1 0 1 0 0 1 1 0 0 0 1 1 1 0 1 1 0 0 1 0 1 1 0

1 0 0 1 1 1 1 1 1 0 0 1 1 1 1 1 1 1 1 1 1 0 1 1 1 0

1 1 0 1 1 1 1 1 0 0 0 1 1 0 1 0 1 1 1 0 1 1 0 1 1 1 0

1 0 0 1 1 1 1 1 1 1 0 1 1 1 1 0 1 0 0 1 1 0 1]

The above series of 0s and 1s are the predicted values for the tumor classes i.e. malignant and benign.

Now, by comparing the two arrays namely **test_labels** and **preds**, we can find out the accuracy of our model. We are going to use the **accuracy_score()** function to determine the accuracy. Consider the following command −

```
from sklearn.metrics import accuracy_score
print(accuracy_score(test_labels,preds))
0.951754385965
```

The result shows that NaïveBayes classifier is 95.17% accurate.

That was machine learning classifier based on the Naïve Bayse Gaussian model.

Support Vector Machines (SVM)

Basically, Support vector machine (SVM) is a supervised machine learning algorithm that can be used for both regression and classification. The main concept of SVM is to plot each data item as a point in n-dimensional space with the value of each feature being the value of a particular coordinate. Here n would be the features we would have. Following is a simple graphical representation to understand the concept of SVM −

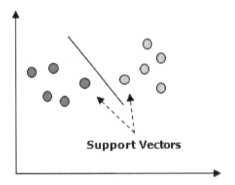

Support Vectors

In the above diagram, we have two features. Hence, we first need to plot these two variables in two dimensional space where each point has two co-ordinates, called support vectors. The line splits the data into two different classified groups. This line would be the classifier.

Here, we are going to build an SVM classifier by using scikit-learn and iris dataset. Scikitlearn library has the **sklearn.svm**module and provides sklearn.svm.svc for classification. The SVM classifier to predict the class of the iris plant based on 4 features are shown below.

Dataset

We will use the iris dataset which contains 3 classes of 50 instances each, where each class refers to a type of iris plant. Each instance has the four features namely sepal length, sepal width, petal length and petal width. The

SVM classifier to predict the class of the iris plant based on 4 features is shown below.

Kernel

It is a technique used by SVM. Basically these are the functions which take low-dimensional input space and transform it to a higher dimensional space. It converts non-separable problem to separable problem. The kernel function can be any one among linear, polynomial, rbf and sigmoid. In this example, we will use the linear kernel.

Let us now import the following packages −

```
import pandas as pd

import numpy as np

from sklearn import svm, datasets

import matplotlib.pyplot as plt
```

Now, load the input data −

```
iris = datasets.load_iris()
```

We are taking first two features −

```
X = iris.data[:, :2]

y = iris.target
```

We will plot the support vector machine boundaries with original data. We are creating a mesh to plot.

```
x_min, x_max = X[:, 0].min() - 1, X[:, 0].max() + 1

y_min, y_max = X[:, 1].min() - 1, X[:, 1].max() + 1

h = (x_max / x_min)/100

xx, yy = np.meshgrid(np.arange(x_min, x_max, h),

np.arange(y_min, y_max, h))

X_plot = np.c_[xx.ravel(), yy.ravel()]
```

We need to give the value of regularization parameter.

```
C = 1.0
```

We need to create the SVM classifier object.

```
Svc_classifier = svm_classifier.SVC(kernel='linear',

C=C, decision_function_shape = 'ovr').fit(X, y)

Z = svc_classifier.predict(X_plot)

Z = Z.reshape(xx.shape)

plt.figure(figsize = (15, 5))

plt.subplot(121)

plt.contourf(xx, yy, Z, cmap = plt.cm.tab10, alpha = 0.3)
```

```
plt.scatter(X[:, 0], X[:, 1], c = y, cmap = plt.cm.Set1)

plt.xlabel('Sepal length')

plt.ylabel('Sepal width')

plt.xlim(xx.min(), xx.max())

plt.title('SVC with linear kernel')
```

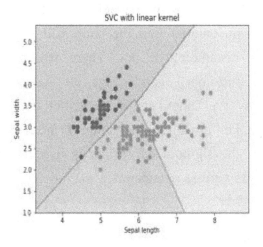

Logistic Regression

Basically, logistic regression model is one of the members of supervised classification algorithm family. Logistic regression measures the relationship between dependent variables and independent variables by estimating the probabilities using a logistic function.

Here, if we talk about dependent and independent variables then dependent variable is the target class variable we are going to predict and on the other side the independent variables are the features we are going to use to predict the target class.

In logistic regression, estimating the probabilities means to predict the likelihood occurrence of the event. For example, the shop owner would like to predict the customer who entered into the shop will buy the play station (for example) or not. There would be many features of customer − gender, age, etc. which would be observed by the shop keeper to predict the likelihood occurrence, i.e., buying a play station or not. The logistic function is the sigmoid curve that is used to build the function with various parameters.

Prerequisites

Before building the classifier using logistic regression, we need to install the Tkinter package on our system. It can be installed

from https://docs.python.org/2/library/tkinter.html.

Now, with the help of the code given below, we can create a classifier using logistic regression −

First, we will import some packages −

```
import numpy as np

from sklearn import linear_model

import matplotlib.pyplot as plt
```

Now, we need to define the sample data which can be done as follows −

```
X = np.array([[2, 4.8], [2.9, 4.7], [2.5, 5], [3.2, 5.5], [6, 5],
[7.6, 4],

        [3.2, 0.9], [2.9, 1.9],[2.4, 3.5], [0.5, 3.4], [1, 4],
[0.9, 5.9]])

y = np.array([0, 0, 0, 1, 1, 1, 2, 2, 2, 3, 3, 3])
```

Next, we need to create the logistic regression classifier, which can be done as follows −

```
Classifier_LR = linear_model.LogisticRegression(solver =
'liblinear', C = 75)
```

Last but not the least, we need to train this classifier −

```
Classifier_LR.fit(X, y)
```

Now, how we can visualize the output? It can be done by creating a function named Logistic_visualize() −

```
Def Logistic_visualize(Classifier_LR, X, y):
  min_x, max_x = X[:, 0].min() - 1.0, X[:, 0].max() + 1.0
  min_y, max_y = X[:, 1].min() - 1.0, X[:, 1].max() + 1.0
```

In the above line, we defined the minimum and maximum values X and Y to be used in mesh grid. In addition, we will define the step size for plotting the mesh grid.

```
mesh_step_size = 0.02
```

Let us define the mesh grid of X and Y values as follows −

```
x_vals, y_vals = np.meshgrid(np.arange(min_x, max_x, mesh_step_size),

        np.arange(min_y, max_y, mesh_step_size))
```

With the help of following code, we can run the classifier on the mesh grid −

```
output      =      classifier.predict(np.c_[x_vals.ravel(), y_vals.ravel()])

output = output.reshape(x_vals.shape)

plt.figure()

plt.pcolormesh(x_vals, y_vals, output, cmap = plt.cm.gray)


plt.scatter(X[:, 0], X[:, 1], c = y, s = 75, edgecolors = 'black',

linewidth=1, cmap = plt.cm.Paired)
```

The following line of code will specify the boundaries of the plot

```
plt.xlim(x_vals.min(), x_vals.max())

plt.ylim(y_vals.min(), y_vals.max())

plt.xticks((np.arange(int(X[:, 0].min() - 1), int(X[:, 0].max()
+ 1), 1.0)))

plt.yticks((np.arange(int(X[:, 1].min() - 1), int(X[:, 1].max()
+ 1), 1.0)))

plt.show()
```

Now, after running the code we will get the following output, logistic regression classifier −

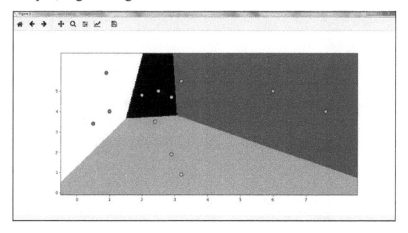

Decision Tree Classifier

A decision tree is basically a binary tree flowchart where each node splits a group of observations according to some feature variable.

Here, we are building a Decision Tree classifier for predicting male or female. We will take a very small data set having 19 samples. These samples would consist of two features – 'height' and 'length of hair'.

Prerequisite

For building the following classifier, we need to install **pydotplus**and **graphviz**. Basically, graphviz is a tool for drawing graphics using dot files and **pydotplus** is a module to Graphviz's Dot language. It can be installed with the package manager or pip.

Now, we can build the decision tree classifier with the help of the following Python code –

To begin with, let us import some important libraries as follows –

```
import pydotplus

from sklearn import tree

from sklearn.datasets import load_iris

from sklearn.metrics import classification_report

from sklearn import cross_validation

import collections
```

Now, we need to provide the dataset as follows –

```
X                                              =
[[165,19],[175,32],[136,35],[174,65],[141,28],[176,15],[13
1,32],

[166,6],[128,32],[179,10],[136,34],[186,2],[126,25],[176,2
8],[112,38],

[169,9],[171,36],[116,25],[196,25]]


Y                                              =
['Man','Woman','Woman','Man','Woman','Man','Woman','M
an','Woman',

'Man','Woman','Man','Woman','Woman','Woman','Man','W
oman','Woman','Man']

data_feature_names = ['height','length of hair']


X_train,     X_test,     Y_train,     Y_test     =
cross_validation.train_test_split

(X, Y, test_size=0.40, random_state=5)
```

After providing the dataset, we need to fit the model which can be done as follows −

```
clf = tree.DecisionTreeClassifier()
clf = clf.fit(X,Y)
```

Prediction can be made with the help of the following Python code −

```
prediction = clf.predict([[133,37]])
print(prediction)
```

We can visualize the decision tree with the help of the following Python code −

```
dot_data   =   tree.export_graphviz(clf,feature_names   =
data_feature_names,
       out_file = None,filled = True,rounded = True)
graph = pydotplus.graph_from_dot_data(dot_data)
colors = ('orange', 'yellow')
edges = collections.defaultdict(list)

for edge in graph.get_edge_list():
edges[edge.get_source()].append(int(edge.get_destination()
))

for edge in edges: edges[edge].sort()

for        i        in        range(2):dest        =
graph.get_node(str(edges[edge][i]))[0]
dest.set_fillcolor(colors[i])
graph.write_png('Decisiontree16.png')
```

It will give the prediction for the above code as **['Woman']** and create the following decision tree −

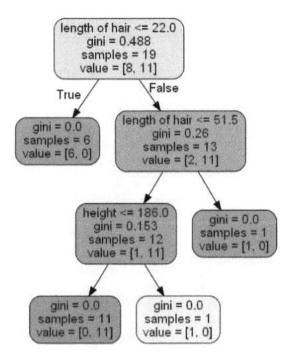

We can change the values of features in prediction to test it.

Random Forest Classifier

As we know that ensemble methods are the methods which combine machine learning models into a more powerful machine learning model. Random Forest, a collection of decision trees, is one of them. It is better than single decision tree because while retaining the predictive powers it can reduce over-fitting by averaging the results.

Here, we are going to implement the random forest model on scikit learn cancer dataset.

Import the necessary packages −

```
from sklearn.ensemble import RandomForestClassifier

from sklearn.model_selection import train_test_split

from sklearn.datasets import load_breast_cancer

cancer = load_breast_cancer()

import matplotlib.pyplot as plt

import numpy as np
```

Now, we need to provide the dataset which can be done as follows &minus

```
cancer = load_breast_cancer()

X_train, X_test, y_train,

y_test  =  train_test_split(cancer.data,  cancer.target,
random_state = 0)
```

After providing the dataset, we need to fit the model which can be done as follows −

```
forest  =  RandomForestClassifier(n_estimators  =  50,
random_state = 0)

forest.fit(X_train,y_train)
```

Now, get the accuracy on training as well as testing subset: if we will increase the number of estimators then, the accuracy of testing subset would also be increased.

```
print('Accuracy          on          the          training
subset:(:.3f)',format(forest.score(X_train,y_train)))

print('Accuracy          on          the          training
subset:(:.3f)',format(forest.score(X_test,y_test)))
```

Output

```
Accuracy on the training subset:(:.3f) 1.0
Accuracy on the training subset:(:.3f) 0.965034965034965
```

Now, like the decision tree, random forest has the **feature_importance** module which will provide a better view of feature weight than decision tree. It can be plot and visualize as follows –

```
n_features = cancer.data.shape[1]

plt.barh(range(n_features),forest.feature_importances_,
align='center')

plt.yticks(np.arange(n_features),cancer.feature_names)

plt.xlabel('Feature Importance')

plt.ylabel('Feature')

plt.show()
```

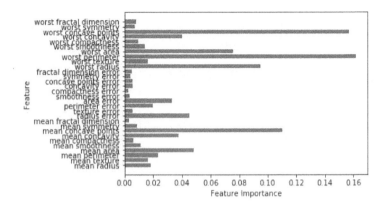

Performance of a classifier

After implementing a machine learning algorithm, we need to find out how effective the model is. The criteria for measuring the effectiveness may be based upon datasets and metric. For evaluating different machine learning algorithms, we can use different performance metrics. For example, suppose if a classifier is used to distinguish between images of different objects, we can use the classification performance metrics such as average accuracy, AUC, etc. In one or other sense, the metric we choose to evaluate our machine learning model is very important because the choice of metrics influences how the performance of a machine learning algorithm is measured and compared. Following are some of the metrics —

Confusion Matrix

Basically it is used for classification problem where the output can be of two or more types of classes. It is the easiest way to measure the performance of a classifier. A confusion matrix is basically a table with two dimensions namely "Actual" and "Predicted". Both the dimensions have "True Positives (TP)", "True Negatives (TN)", "False Positives (FP)", "False Negatives (FN)".

	Actual 1	0
Predicted 1	True Positives (TP)	False Positives (FP)
0	False Negatives (FN)	True Negatives (TN)

Confusion Matrix

In the confusion matrix above, 1 is for positive class and 0 is for negative class.

Following are the terms associated with Confusion matrix –

- **True Positives** – TPs are the cases when the actual class of data point was 1 and the predicted is also 1.

- **True Negatives** – TNs are the cases when the actual class of the data point was 0 and the predicted is also 0.

- **False Positives** − FPs are the cases when the actual class of data point was 0 and the predicted is also 1.

- **False Negatives** − FNs are the cases when the actual class of the data point was 1 and the predicted is also 0.

Accuracy

The confusion matrix itself is not a performance measure as such but almost all the performance matrices are based on the confusion matrix. One of them is accuracy. In classification problems, it may be defined as the number of correct predictions made by the model over all kinds of predictions made. The formula for calculating the accuracy is as follows −

Accuracy=TP+TNTP+FP+FN+TNAccuracy=TP+TNTP+FP+FN+TN

Precision

It is mostly used in document retrievals. It may be defined as how many of the returned documents are correct. Following is the formula for calculating the precision −

Precision=TPTP+FPPrecision=TPTP+FP

Recall or Sensitivity

It may be defined as how many of the positives do the model return. Following is the formula for calculating the recall/sensitivity of the model −

Recall=TPTP+FNRecall=TPTP+FN

Specificity

It may be defined as how many of the negatives do the model return. It is exactly opposite to recall. Following is the formula for calculating the specificity of the model −

Specificity=TNTN+FPSpecificity=TNTN+FP

Class Imbalance Problem

Class imbalance is the scenario where the number of observations belonging to one class is significantly lower than those belonging to the other classes. For example, this problem is prominent in the scenario where we need to identify the rare diseases, fraudulent transactions in bank etc.

Example of imbalanced classes

Let us consider an example of fraud detection data set to understand the concept of imbalanced class −

Total observations = 5000

Fraudulent Observations = 50

Non-Fraudulent Observations = 4950

Event Rate = 1%

Solution

Balancing the classes' acts as a solution to imbalanced classes. The main objective of balancing the classes is to either increase the frequency of the minority class or decrease the frequency of the majority class.

Following are the approaches to solve the issue of imbalances classes −

Re-Sampling

Re-sampling is a series of methods used to reconstruct the sample data sets − both training sets and testing sets. Re-sampling is done to improve the accuracy of model. Following are some re-sampling techniques −

- **Random Under-Sampling** − This technique aims to balance class distribution by randomly eliminating majority class examples. This is done until the majority and minority class instances are balanced out.

Total observations = 5000

Fraudulent Observations = 50

Non-Fraudulent Observations = 4950

Event Rate = 1%

In this case, we are taking 10% samples without replacement from non-fraud instances and then combine them with the fraud instances −

Non-fraudulent observations after random under sampling = 10% of 4950 = 495

Total observations after combining them with fraudulent observations = 50+495 = 545

Hence now, the event rate for new dataset after under sampling = 9%

The main advantage of this technique is that it can reduce run time and improve storage. But on the other side, it can discard useful information while reducing the number of training data samples.

- **Random Over-Sampling** − This technique aims to balance class distribution by increasing the number of instances in the minority class by replicating them.

Total observations = 5000

Fraudulent Observations = 50

Non-Fraudulent Observations = 4950

Event Rate = 1%

In case we are replicating 50 fraudulent observations 30 times then fraudulent observations after replicating the minority class observations would be 1500. And then total observations in the new data after oversampling would be 4950+1500 = 6450. Hence the event rate for the new data set would be 1500/6450 = 23%.

The main advantage of this method is that there would be no loss of useful information. But on the other hand, it has the increased chances of over-fitting because it replicates the minority class events.

Ensemble Techniques

This methodology basically is used to modify existing classification algorithms to make them appropriate for imbalanced data sets. In this approach we construct several two stage classifier from the original data and then aggregate their predictions. Random forest classifier is an example of ensemble based classifier.

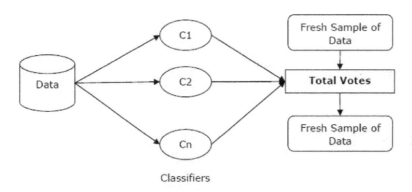

Ensemble based Methodology

AI with Python – Supervised Learning: Regression

Regression is one of the most important statistical and machine learning tools. We would not be wrong to say that the journey of machine learning starts from regression. It may be defined as the parametric technique that allows us to make decisions based upon data or in other words allows us to make predictions based upon data by learning the relationship between input and output variables. Here, the output variables dependent on the input variables, are continuous-valued real numbers. In regression, the relationship between input and output variables matters and it helps us in understanding how the value of the output variable changes with the change of input variable. Regression is frequently used for prediction of prices, economics, variations, and so on

.

Building Regressors in Python:

In this section, we will learn how to build single as well as multivariable regressor.

Linear Regressor/Single Variable Regressor

Let us important a few required packages −

```
import numpy as np

from sklearn import linear_model
```

```
import sklearn.metrics as sm

import matplotlib.pyplot as plt
```

Now, we need to provide the input data and we have saved our data in the file named linear.txt.

```
input = 'D:/ProgramData/linear.txt'
```

We need to load this data by using the **np.loadtxt** function.

```
input_data = np.loadtxt(input, delimiter=',')

X, y = input_data[:, :-1], input_data[:, -1]
```

The next step would be to train the model. Let us give training and testing samples.

```
training_samples = int(0.6 * len(X))

testing_samples = len(X) - num_training
```

```
X_train,      y_train      =      X[:training_samples],
y[:training_samples]
```

```
X_test, y_test = X[training_samples:], y[training_samples:]
```

Now, we need to create a linear regressor object.

```
reg_linear = linear_model.LinearRegression()
```

Train the object with the training samples.

```
reg_linear.fit(X_train, y_train)
```

We need to do the prediction with the testing data.

```
y_test_pred = reg_linear.predict(X_test)
```

Now plot and visualize the data.

```
plt.scatter(X_test, y_test, color = 'red')
plt.plot(X_test, y_test_pred, color = 'black', linewidth = 2)
plt.xticks(())
plt.yticks(())
plt.show()
```

Output:

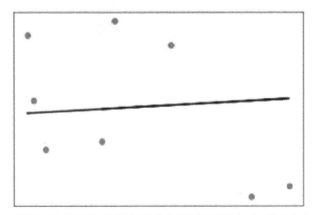

Now, we can compute the performance of our linear regression as follows −

```
print("Performance of Linear regressor:")

print("Mean                absolute                error               =",
round(sm.mean_absolute_error(y_test, y_test_pred), 2))

print("Mean                squared                error               =",
round(sm.mean_squared_error(y_test, y_test_pred), 2))

print("Median              absolute                error               =",
round(sm.median_absolute_error(y_test, y_test_pred), 2))

print("Explain             variance                score               =",
round(sm.explained_variance_score(y_test, y_test_pred),

2))

print("R2 score =", round(sm.r2_score(y_test, y_test_pred),
2))
```

Performance of Linear Regressor –

Mean absolute error = 1.78
Mean squared error = 3.89
Median absolute error = 2.01
Explain variance score = -0.09
R2 score = -0.09

In the above code, we have used this small data. If you want some big dataset then you can use sklearn.dataset to import bigger dataset.

2,4.82.9,4.72.5,53.2,5.56,57.6,43.2,0.92.9,1.92.4,

3.50.5,3.41,40.9,5.91.2,2.583.2,5.65.1,1.54.5,

1.22.3,6.32.1,2.8

Multivariable Regressor

First, let us import a few required packages –

import numpy as np

from sklearn import linear_model

import sklearn.metrics as sm

import matplotlib.pyplot as plt

from sklearn.preprocessing import PolynomialFeatures

Now, we need to provide the input data and we have saved our data in the file named linear.txt.

```
input = 'D:/ProgramData/Mul_linear.txt'
```

We will load this data by using the **np.loadtxt** function.

```
input_data = np.loadtxt(input, delimiter=',')
X, y = input_data[:, :-1], input_data[:, -1]
```

The next step would be to train the model; we will give training and testing samples.

```
training_samples = int(0.6 * len(X))
testing_samples = len(X) - num_training
```

```
X_train,       y_train       =       X[:training_samples],
y[:training_samples]
```

```
X_test, y_test = X[training_samples:], y[training_samples:]
```

Now, we need to create a linear regressor object.

```
reg_linear_mul = linear_model.LinearRegression()
```

Train the object with the training samples.

```
reg_linear_mul.fit(X_train, y_train)
```

Now, at last we need to do the prediction with the testing data.

```
y_test_pred = reg_linear_mul.predict(X_test)

print("Performance of Linear regressor:")
print("Mean              absolute              error              =",
round(sm.mean_absolute_error(y_test, y_test_pred), 2))
print("Mean              squared               error              =",
round(sm.mean_squared_error(y_test, y_test_pred), 2))
print("Median            absolute              error              =",
round(sm.median_absolute_error(y_test, y_test_pred), 2))
print("Explain           variance              score              =",
round(sm.explained_variance_score(y_test,   y_test_pred),
2))
print("R2 score =", round(sm.r2_score(y_test, y_test_pred),
2))
```

Output:

Performance of Linear Regressor −

```
Mean absolute error = 0.6
Mean squared error = 0.65
Median absolute error = 0.41
Explain variance score = 0.34
R2 score = 0.33
```

Now, we will create a polynomial of degree 10 and train the regressor. We will provide the sample data point.

```
polynomial = PolynomialFeatures(degree = 10)

X_train_transformed = polynomial.fit_transform(X_train)

datapoint = [[2.23, 1.35, 1.12]]

poly_datapoint = polynomial.fit_transform(datapoint)


poly_linear_model = linear_model.LinearRegression()

poly_linear_model.fit(X_train_transformed, y_train)

print("\nLinear                    regression:\n",
reg_linear_mul.predict(datapoint))

print("\nPolynomial                regression:\n",
poly_linear_model.predict(poly_datapoint))
```

Output:

Linear regression −

[2.40170462]

Polynomial regression −

[1.8697225]

In the above code, we have used this small data. If you want a big dataset then, you can use sklearn.dataset to import a bigger dataset.

2,4.8,1.2,3.22.9,4.7,1.5,3.62.5,5,2.8,23.2,5.5,3.5,2.16,5,

2,3.27.6,4,1.2,3.23.2,0.9,2.3,1.42.9,1.9,2.3,1.22.4,3.5,

2.8,3.60.5,3.4,1.8,2.91,4,3,2.50.9,5.9,5.6,0.81.2,2.58,

3.45,1.233.2,5.6,2,3.25.1,1.5,1.2,1.34.5,1.2,4.1,2.32.3,

6.3,2.5,3.22.1,2.8,1.2,3.6

AI with Python – Logic Programming

In this chapter, we will focus logic programming and how it helps in Artificial Intelligence.

We already know that logic is the study of principles of correct reasoning or in simple words it is the study of what comes after what. For example, if two statements are true then we can infer any third statement from it.

Concept:

Logic Programming is the combination of two words, logic and programming. Logic Programming is a programming paradigm in which the problems are expressed as facts and rules by program statements but within a system of formal logic. Just like other programming paradigms like object oriented, functional, declarative, and procedural, etc., it is also a particular way to approach programming.

How to Solve Problems with Logic Programming

Logic Programming uses facts and rules for solving the problem. That is why they are called the building blocks of Logic Programming. A goal needs to be specified for every program in logic programming. To understand how a problem can be solved in logic programming, we need to know about the building blocks − Facts and Rules −

Facts

Actually, every logic program needs facts to work with so that it can achieve the given goal. Facts basically are true statements about the program and data. For example, Delhi is the capital of India.

Rules

Actually, rules are the constraints which allow us to make conclusions about the problem domain. Rules basically written as logical clauses to express various facts. For example, if we are building any game then all the rules must be defined.

Rules are very important to solve any problem in Logic Programming. Rules are basically logical conclusion which can express the facts. Following is the syntax of rule −

A:− B1,B2,...,B$_n$.

Here, A is the head and B1, B2, ... Bn is the body.

For example − ancestor(X,Y) :- father(X,Y).

ancestor(X,Z) :- father(X,Y), ancestor(Y,Z).

This can be read as, for every X and Y, if X is the father of Y and Y is an ancestor of Z, X is the ancestor of Z. For every X and Y, X is the ancestor of Z, if X is the father of Y and Y is an ancestor of Z.

Installing Useful Packages:

For starting logic programming in Python, we need to install the following two packages –

Kanren

It provides us a way to simplify the way we made code for business logic. It lets us express the logic in terms of rules and facts. The following command will help you install kanren –

```
pip install kanren
```

SymPy

SymPy is a Python library for symbolic mathematics. It aims to become a full-featured computer algebra system (CAS) while keeping the code as simple as possible in order to be comprehensible and easily extensible. The following command will help you install SymPy –

```
pip install sympy
```

Examples of Logic Programming:

Followings are some examples which can be solved by logic programming –

Matching mathematical expressions

Actually we can find the unknown values by using logic programming in a very effective way. The following Python code will help you match a mathematical expression –

Consider importing the following packages first –

```
from kanren import run, var, fact

from kanren.assoccomm import eq_assoccomm as eq

from kanren.assoccomm import commutative, associative
```

We need to define the mathematical operations which we are going to use –

```
add = 'add'

mul = 'mul'
```

Both addition and multiplication are communicative processes. Hence, we need to specify it and this can be done as follows –

```
fact(commutative, mul)

fact(commutative, add)

fact(associative, mul)

fact(associative, add)
```

It is compulsory to define variables; this can be done as follows −

```
a, b = var('a'), var('b')
```

We need to match the expression with the original pattern. We have the following original pattern, which is basically (5+a)*b −

```
Original_pattern = (mul, (add, 5, a), b)
```

We have the following two expressions to match with the original pattern −

```
exp1 = (mul, 2, (add, 3, 1))

exp2 = (add,5,(mul,8,1))
```

Output can be printed with the following command −

```
print(run(0, (a,b), eq(original_pattern, exp1)))
print(run(0, (a,b), eq(original_pattern, exp2)))
```

After running this code, we will get the following output −

```
((3,2))
()
```

The first output represents the values for **a** and **b**. The first expression matched the original pattern and returned the values for **a** and **b** but the second expression did not match the original pattern hence nothing has been returned.

Checking for Prime Numbers

With the help of logic programming, we can find the prime numbers from a list of numbers and can also generate prime numbers. The Python code given below will find the prime number from a list of numbers and will also generate the first 10 prime numbers.

Let us first consider importing the following packages −

```python
from kanren import isvar, run, membero

from kanren.core import success, fail, goaleval, condeseq, eq, var

from sympy.ntheory.generate import prime, isprime

import itertools as it
```

Now, we will define a function called prime_check which will check the prime numbers based on the given numbers as data.

```
def prime_check(x):

if isvar(x):

    return    condeseq([[(eq,x,p)]    for    p    in    map(prime,
it.count(1)))

else:

    return success if isprime(x) else fail
```

Now, we need to declare a variable which will be used −

```
x = var()

print((set(run(0,x,(membero,x,(12,14,15,19,20,21,22,23,29,
30,41,44,52,62,65,85)),

(prime_check,x)))))

print((run(10,x,prime_check(x))))
```

The output of the above code will be as follows −

```
{19, 23, 29, 41}
(2, 3, 5, 7, 11, 13, 17, 19, 23, 29)
```

Solving Puzzles

Logic programming can be used to solve many problems like 8-puzzles, Zebra puzzle, Sudoku, N-queen, etc. Here we are taking an example of a variant of Zebra puzzle which is as follows −

There are five houses.

The English man lives in the red house.

The Swede has a dog.

The Dane drinks tea.

The green house is immediately to the left of the white house.

They drink coffee in the green house.

The man who smokes Pall Mall has birds.

In the yellow house they smoke Dunhill.

In the middle house they drink milk.

The Norwegian lives in the first house.

The man who smokes Blend lives in the house next to the house with cats.

In a house next to the house where they have a horse, they smoke Dunhill.

The man who smokes Blue Master drinks beer.

The German smokes Prince.

The Norwegian lives next to the blue house.

They drink water in a house next to the house where they smoke Blend.

We are solving it for the question **who owns zebra** with the help of Python.

Let us import the necessary packages −

```
from kanren import *

from kanren.core import lall

import time
```

Now, we need to define two functions − **left()** and **next()** to check whose house is left or next to who's house −

```
def left(q, p, list):

  return membero((q,p), zip(list, list[1:]))

def next(q, p, list):

  return conde([left(q, p, list)], [left(p, q, list)])
```

Now, we will declare a variable house as follows −

```
houses = var()
```

We need to define the rules with the help of lall package as follows.

There are 5 houses −

```
rules_zebraproblem = lall(
```

(eq, (var(), var(), var(), var(), var()), houses),

(membero,('Englishman', var(), var(), var(), 'red'), houses),

(membero,('Swede', var(), var(), 'dog', var()), houses),

(membero,('Dane', var(), 'tea', var(), var()), houses),

(left,(var(), var(), var(), var(), 'green'),

(var(), var(), var(), var(), 'white'), houses),

(membero,(var(), var(), 'coffee', var(), 'green'), houses),

(membero,(var(), 'Pall Mall', var(), 'birds', var()), houses),

(membero,(var(), 'Dunhill', var(), var(), 'yellow'), houses),

(eq,(var(), var(), (var(), var(), 'milk', var(), var()), var(), var()), houses),

(eq,(('Norwegian', var(), var(), var(), var()), var(), var(), var(), var()), houses),

(next,(var(), 'Blend', var(), var(), var()),

(var(), var(), var(), 'cats', var()), houses),

(next,(var(), 'Dunhill', var(), var(), var()),

(var(), var(), var(), 'horse', var()), houses),

(membero,(var(), 'Blue Master', 'beer', var(), var()), houses),

```
    (membero,('German', 'Prince', var(), var(), var()), houses),

    (next,('Norwegian', var(), var(), var(), var())),

    (var(), var(), var(), var(), 'blue'), houses),

    (next,(var(), 'Blend', var(), var(), var())),

    (var(), var(), 'water', var(), var()), houses),

    (membero,(var(), var(), var(), 'zebra', var()), houses)
)
```

Now, run the solver with the preceding constraints −

```
solutions = run(0, houses, rules_zebraproblem)
```

With the help of the following code, we can extract the output from the solver −

```
output_zebra = [house for house in solutions[0] if 'zebra' in house][0][0]
```

The following code will help print the solution −

```
print ('\n'+ output_zebra + 'owns zebra.')
```

The output of the above code would be as follows −

```
German owns zebra.
```

AI with Python - Unsupervised Learning: Clustering

Unsupervised machine learning algorithms do not have any supervisor to provide any sort of guidance. That is why they are closely aligned with what some call true artificial intelligence.

In unsupervised learning, there would be no correct answer and no teacher for the guidance. Algorithms need to discover the interesting pattern in data for learning.

What is Clustering?

Basically, it is a type of unsupervised learning method and a common technique for statistical data analysis used in many fields. Clustering mainly is a task of dividing the set of observations into subsets, called clusters, in such a way that observations in the same cluster are similar in one sense and they are dissimilar to the observations in other clusters. In simple words, we can say that the main goal of clustering is to group the data on the basis of similarity and dissimilarity.

For example, the following diagram shows similar kind of data in different clusters −

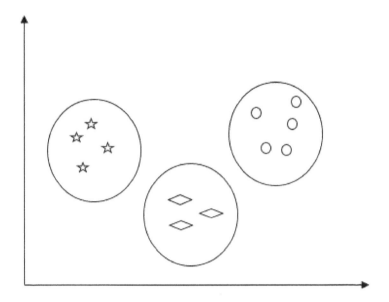

Algorithms for Clustering the Data:

Following are a few common algorithms for clustering the data –

K-Means algorithm

K-means clustering algorithm is one of the well-known algorithms for clustering the data. We need to assume that the numbers of clusters are already known. This is also called flat clustering. It is an iterative clustering algorithm. The steps given below need to be followed for this algorithm –

Step 1 – We need to specify the desired number of K subgroups.

Step 2 − Fix the number of clusters and randomly assign each data point to a cluster. Or in other words we need to classify our data based on the number of clusters.

In this step, cluster centroids should be computed.

As this is an iterative algorithm, we need to update the locations of K centroids with every iteration until we find the global optima or in other words the centroids reach at their optimal locations.

The following code will help in implementing K-means clustering algorithm in Python. We are going to use the Scikit-learn module.

Let us import the necessary packages −

```
import matplotlib.pyplot as plt

import seaborn as sns; sns.set()

import numpy as np

from sklearn.cluster import KMeans
```

The following line of code will help in generating the two-dimensional dataset, containing four blobs, by using **make_blob** from the **sklearn.dataset** package.

```
from        sklearn.datasets.samples_generator        import
make_blobs
```

X, y_true = make_blobs(n_samples = 500, centers = 4,

cluster_std = 0.40, random_state = 0)

We can visualize the dataset by using the following code −

plt.scatter(X[:, 0], X[:, 1], s = 50);

plt.show()

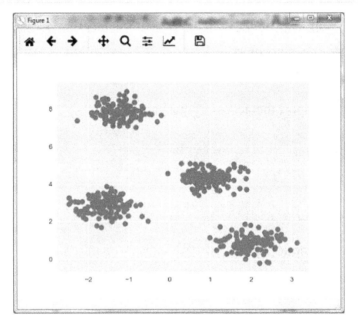

Here, we are initializing kmeans to be the KMeans algorithm, with the required parameter of how many clusters (n_clusters).

```
kmeans = KMeans(n_clusters = 4)
```

We need to train the K-means model with the input data.

```
kmeans.fit(X)

y_kmeans = kmeans.predict(X)

plt.scatter(X[:, 0], X[:, 1], c = y_kmeans, s = 50, cmap =
'viridis')


centers = kmeans.cluster_centers_
```

The code given below will help us plot and visualize the machine's findings based on our data, and the fitment according to the number of clusters that are to be found.

```
plt.scatter(centers[:, 0], centers[:, 1], c = 'black', s = 200,
alpha = 0.5);

plt.show()
```

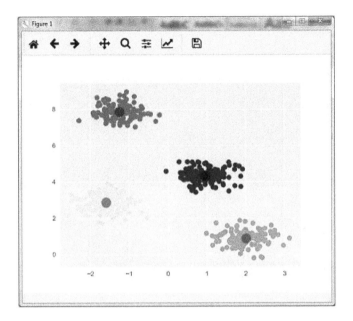

Mean Shift Algorithm

It is another popular and powerful clustering algorithm used in unsupervised learning. It does not make any assumptions hence it is a non-parametric algorithm. It is also called hierarchical clustering or mean shift cluster analysis. Followings would be the basic steps of this algorithm −

- First of all, we need to start with the data points assigned to a cluster of their own.

- Now, it computes the centroids and update the location of new centroids.

- By repeating this process, we move closer the peak of cluster i.e. towards the region of higher density.

- This algorithm stops at the stage where centroids do not move anymore.

With the help of following code we are implementing Mean Shift clustering algorithm in Python. We are going to use Scikit-learn module.

Let us import the necessary packages −

```
import numpy as np

from sklearn.cluster import MeanShift

import matplotlib.pyplot as plt

from matplotlib import style

style.use("ggplot")
```

The following code will help in generating the two-dimensional dataset, containing four blobs, by using **make_blob** from the **sklearn.dataset** package.

```
from      sklearn.datasets.samples_generator      import
make_blobs
```

We can visualize the dataset with the following code

```
centers = [[2,2],[4,5],[3,10]]

X, _ = make_blobs(n_samples = 500, centers = centers,
cluster_std = 1)

plt.scatter(X[:,0],X[:,1])

plt.show()
```

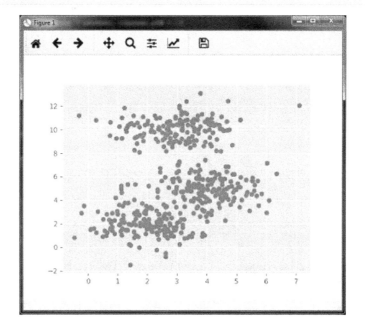

Now, we need to train the Mean Shift cluster model with the input data.

```
ms = MeanShift()

ms.fit(X)

labels = ms.labels_

cluster_centers = ms.cluster_centers_
```

The following code will print the cluster centers and the expected number of cluster as per the input data −

```
print(cluster_centers)

n_clusters_ = len(np.unique(labels))

print("Estimated clusters:", n_clusters_)

[[ 3.23005036 3.84771893]

[ 3.02057451 9.88928991]]

Estimated clusters: 2
```

The code given below will help plot and visualize the machine's findings based on our data, and the fitment according to the number of clusters that are to be found.

```
colors = 10*['r.','g.','b.','c.','k.','y.','m.']

  for i in range(len(X)):

  plt.plot(X[i][0], X[i][1], colors[labels[i]], markersize = 10)

plt.scatter(cluster_centers[:,0],cluster_centers[:,1],
```

```
    marker = "x",color = 'k', s = 150, linewidths = 5, zorder =
10)

plt.show()
```

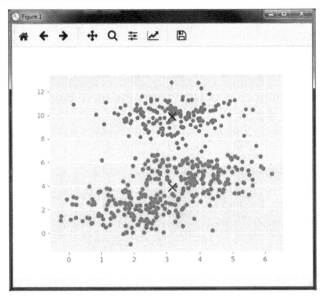

Measuring the Clustering Performance:

The real world data is not naturally organized into number of distinctive clusters. Due to this reason, it is not easy to visualize and draw inferences. That is why we need to measure the clustering performance as well as its quality. It can be done with the help of silhouette analysis.

Silhouette Analysis

This method can be used to check the quality of clustering by measuring the distance between the clusters. Basically, it provides a way to assess the parameters like number of clusters by giving a silhouette score. This score is a metric that measures how close each point in one cluster is to the points in the neighboring clusters.

Analysis of silhouette score

The score has a range of [-1, 1]. Following is the analysis of this score −

- **Score of +1** − Score near +1 indicates that the sample is far away from the neighboring cluster.

- **Score of 0** − Score 0 indicates that the sample is on or very close to the decision boundary between two neighboring clusters.

- **Score of -1** − Negative score indicates that the samples have been assigned to the wrong clusters.

Calculating Silhouette Score

In this section, we will learn how to calculate the silhouette score.

Silhouette score can be calculated by using the following formula −

silhouettescore=(p−q)max(p,q)silhouettescore=(p−q)max(p ,q)

Here, p is the mean distance to the points in the nearest cluster that the data point is not a part of. And, q is the mean intra-cluster distance to all the points in its own cluster.

For finding the optimal number of clusters, we need to run the clustering algorithm again by importing the **metrics** module from the **sklearn** package. In the following example, we will run the K-means clustering algorithm to find the optimal number of clusters −

Import the necessary packages as shown −

import matplotlib.pyplot as plt

import seaborn as sns; sns.set()

import numpy as np

from sklearn.cluster import KMeans

With the help of the following code, we will generate the two-dimensional dataset, containing four blobs, by using **make_blob** from the **sklearn.dataset** package.

from sklearn.datasets.samples_generator import make_blobs

```
X, y_true = make_blobs(n_samples = 500, centers = 4,
cluster_std = 0.40, random_state = 0)
```

Initialize the variables as shown −

```
scores = []

values = np.arange(2, 10)
```

We need to iterate the K-means model through all the values and also need to train it with the input data.

```
for num_clusters in values:

kmeans = KMeans(init = 'k-means++', n_clusters =
num_clusters, n_init = 10)

kmeans.fit(X)
```

Now, estimate the silhouette score for the current clustering model using the Euclidean distance metric −

```
score = metrics.silhouette_score(X, kmeans.labels_,

metric = 'euclidean', sample_size = len(X))
```

The following line of code will help in displaying the number of clusters as well as Silhouette score.

```
print("\nNumber of clusters =", num_clusters)

print("Silhouette score =", score)
```

```
scores.append(score)
```

You will receive the following output −

```
Number of clusters = 9
Silhouette score = 0.340391138371
```

```
num_clusters = np.argmax(scores) + values[0]
print('\nOptimal number of clusters =', num_clusters)
```

Now, the output for optimal number of clusters would be as follows −

Optimal number of clusters = 2

Finding Nearest Neighbors

If we want to build recommender systems such as a movie recommender system then we need to understand the concept of finding the nearest neighbors. It is because the recommender system utilizes the concept of nearest neighbors.

The **concept of finding nearest neighbors** may be defined as the process of finding the closest point to the input point from the given dataset. The main use of this KNN)K-nearest neighbors) algorithm is to build classification systems that classify a data point on the proximity of the input data point to various classes.

The Python code given below helps in finding the K-nearest neighbors of a given data set —

Import the necessary packages as shown below. Here, we are using the **NearestNeighbors** module from the **sklearn** package

```
import numpy as np

import matplotlib.pyplot as plt

from sklearn.neighbors import NearestNeighbors
```

Let us now define the input data —

```
A = np.array([[3.1, 2.3], [2.3, 4.2], [3.9, 3.5], [3.7, 6.4],
[4.8, 1.9],

        [8.3, 3.1], [5.2, 7.5], [4.8, 4.7], [3.5, 5.1], [4.4,
2.9],])
```

Now, we need to define the nearest neighbors —

```
k = 3
```

We also need to give the test data from which the nearest neighbors is to be found —

```
test_data = [3.3, 2.9]
```

The following code can visualize and plot the input data defined by us —

```
plt.figure()

plt.title('Input data')

plt.scatter(A[:,0], A[:,1], marker = 'o', s = 100, color = 'black')
```

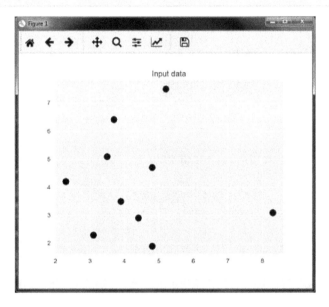

Now, we need to build the K Nearest Neighbor. The object also needs to be trained

```
knn_model = NearestNeighbors(n_neighbors = k, algorithm = 'auto').fit(X)

distances, indices = knn_model.kneighbors([test_data])
```

Now, we can print the K nearest neighbors as follows

```
print("\nK Nearest Neighbors:")

for rank, index in enumerate(indices[0][:k], start = 1):

    print(str(rank) + " is", A[index])
```

We can visualize the nearest neighbors along with the test data point

```
plt.figure()

plt.title('Nearest neighbors')

plt.scatter(A[:, 0], X[:, 1], marker = 'o', s = 100, color = 'k')

plt.scatter(A[indices][0][:][:, 0], A[indices][0][:][:, 1],

    marker = 'o', s = 250, color = 'k', facecolors = 'none')

plt.scatter(test_data[0], test_data[1],

    marker = 'x', s = 100, color = 'k')

plt.show()
```

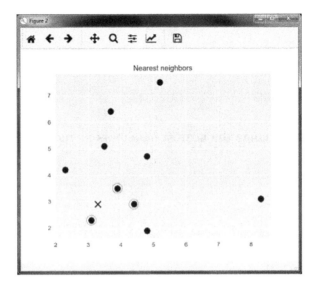

Output:

K Nearest Neighbors

```
1 is [ 3.1 2.3]
2 is [ 3.9 3.5]
3 is [ 4.4 2.9]
```

K-Nearest Neighbors Classifier

A K-Nearest Neighbors (KNN) classifier is a classification model that uses the nearest neighbors algorithm to classify a given data point. We have implemented the KNN algorithm in the last section, now we are going to build a KNN classifier using that algorithm.

Concept of KNN Classifier:

The basic concept of K-nearest neighbor classification is to find a predefined number, i.e., the 'k' − of training samples closest in distance to a new sample, which has to be classified. New samples will get their label from the neighbors itself. The KNN classifiers have a fixed user defined constant for the number of neighbors which have to be determined. For the distance, standard Euclidean distance is the most common choice. The KNN Classifier works directly on the learned samples rather than creating the rules for learning. The KNN algorithm is among the simplest of all machine learning algorithms. It has been quite successful in a large number of classification and regression problems, for example, character recognition or image analysis.

Example

We are building a KNN classifier to recognize digits. For this, we will use the MNIST dataset. We will write this code in the Jupyter Notebook.

Import the necessary packages as shown below.

Here we are using the **KNeighborsClassifier** module from the **sklearn.neighbors** package −

```
from sklearn.datasets import *

import pandas as pd

%matplotlib inline

from sklearn.neighbors import KNeighborsClassifier

import matplotlib.pyplot as plt

import numpy as np
```

The following code will display the image of digit to verify what image we have to test −

```
def Image_display(i):

    plt.imshow(digit['images'][i],cmap = 'Greys_r')

    plt.show()
```

Now, we need to load the MNIST dataset. Actually there are total 1797 images but we are using the first 1600 images as training sample and the remaining 197 would be kept for testing purpose.

```
digit = load_digits()

digit_d = pd.DataFrame(digit['data'][0:1600])
```

Now, on displaying the images we can see the output as follows −

Image_display(0)

Image_display(0)

Image of 0 is displayed as follows −

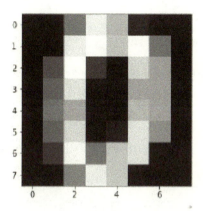

Image_display(9)

Image of 9 is displayed as follows −

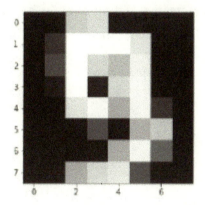

digit.keys()

Now, we need to create the training and testing data set and supply testing data set to the KNN classifiers.

```
train_x = digit['data'][:1600]

train_y = digit['target'][:1600]

KNN = KNeighborsClassifier(20)

KNN.fit(train_x,train_y)
```

The following output will create the K nearest neighbor classifier constructor −

```
KNeighborsClassifier(algorithm = 'auto', leaf_size = 30, metric = 'minkowski',
   metric_params = None, n_jobs = 1, n_neighbors = 20, p = 2,
   weights = 'uniform')
```

We need to create the testing sample by providing any arbitrary number greater than 1600, which were the training samples.

```
test = np.array(digit['data'][1725])

test1 = test.reshape(1,-1)

Image_display(1725)
```

```
Image_display(6)
```

Image of 6 is displayed as follows −

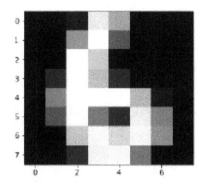

Now we will predict the test data as follows −

```
KNN.predict(test1)
```

The above code will generate the following output −

```
array([6])
```

Now, consider the following −

```
digit['target_names']
```

The above code will generate the following output −

```
array([0, 1, 2, 3, 4, 5, 6, 7, 8, 9])
```

AI with Python – Natural Language Processing

Natural Language Processing (NLP) refers to AI method of communicating with intelligent systems using a natural language such as English.

Processing of Natural Language is required when you want an intelligent system like robot to perform as per your instructions, when you want to hear decision from a dialogue based clinical expert system, etc.

The field of NLP involves making computers erform useful tasks with the natural languages humans use. The input and output of an NLP system can be −

- Speech
- Written Text

Components of NLP

In this section, we will learn about the different components of NLP. There are two components of NLP. The components are described below −

Natural Language Understanding (NLU)

It involves the following tasks −

- Mapping the given input in natural language into useful representations.

- Analyzing different aspects of the language.

Natural Language Generation (NLG)

It is the process of producing meaningful phrases and sentences in the form of natural language from some internal representation. It involves −

- **Text planning** − This includes retrieving the relevant content from the knowledge base.

- **Sentence planning** − This includes choosing the required words, forming meaningful phrases, setting tone of the sentence.

- **Text Realization** − This is mapping sentence plan into sentence structure.

Difficulties in NLU

The NLU is very rich in form and structure; however, it is ambiguous. There can be different levels of ambiguity −

Lexical ambiguity

It is at a very primitive level such as the word-level. For example, treating the word "board" as noun or verb?

Syntax level ambiguity

A sentence can be parsed in different ways. For example, "He lifted the beetle with red cap." – Did he use cap to lift the beetle or he lifted a beetle that had red cap?

Referential ambiguity

Referring to something using pronouns. For example, Rima went to Gauri. She said, "I am tired." – Exactly who is tired?

NLP Terminology

Let us now see a few important terms in the NLP terminology.

- **Phonology** – It is study of organizing sound systematically.

- **Morphology** – It is a study of construction of words from primitive meaningful units.

- **Morpheme** – It is a primitive unit of meaning in a language.

- **Syntax** – It refers to arranging words to make a sentence. It also involves determining the structural role of words in the sentence and in phrases.

- **Semantics** – It is concerned with the meaning of words and how to combine words into meaningful phrases and sentences.

- **Pragmatics** – It deals with using and understanding sentences in different situations and how the interpretation of the sentence is affected.

- **Discourse** – It deals with how the immediately preceding sentence can affect the interpretation of the next sentence.

- **World Knowledge** – It includes the general knowledge about the world.

Steps in NLP:

This section shows the different steps in NLP.

Lexical Analysis

It involves identifying and analyzing the structure of words. Lexicon of a language means the collection of words and phrases in a language. Lexical analysis is dividing the whole chunk of txt into paragraphs, sentences, and words.

Syntactic Analysis (Parsing)

It involves analysis of words in the sentence for grammar and arranging words in a manner that shows the relationship among the words. The sentence such as "The school goes to boy" is rejected by English syntactic analyzer.

Semantic Analysis

It draws the exact meaning or the dictionary meaning from the text. The text is checked for meaningfulness. It is done by mapping syntactic structures and objects in the task domain. The semantic analyzer disregards sentence such as "hot ice-cream".

Discourse Integration

The meaning of any sentence depends upon the meaning of the sentence just before it. In addition, it also brings about the meaning of immediately succeeding sentence.

Pragmatic Analysis

During this, what was said is re-interpreted on what it actually meant. It involves deriving those aspects of language which require real world knowledge.

AI with Python – NLTK Package

In this chapter, we will learn how to get started with the Natural Language Toolkit Package.

Prerequisite

If we want to build applications with Natural Language processing then the change in context makes it most difficult. The context factor influences how the machine understands a particular sentence. Hence, we need to develop Natural language applications by using machine learning approaches so that machine can also understand the way a human can understand the context.

To build such applications we will use the Python package called NLTK (Natural Language Toolkit Package).

Importing NLTK

We need to install NLTK before using it. It can be installed with the help of the following command −

```
pip install nltk
```

To build a conda package for NLTK, use the following command −

```
conda install -c anaconda nltk
```

Now after installing the NLTK package, we need to import it through the python command prompt. We can import it by writing the following command on the Python command prompt −

```
>>> import nltk
```

Downloading NLTK's Data

Now after importing NLTK, we need to download the required data. It can be done with the help of the following command on the Python command prompt −

```
>>> nltk.download()
```

Installing Other Necessary Packages

For building natural language processing applications by using NLTK, we need to install the necessary packages. The packages are as follows −

gensim

It is a robust semantic modeling library that is useful for many applications. We can install it by executing the following command −

```
pip install gensim
```

pattern

It is used to make **gensim** package work properly. We can install it by executing the following command

```
pip install pattern
```

Concept of Tokenization, Stemming, and Lemmatization:

In this section, we will understand what is tokenization, stemming, and lemmatization.

Tokenization

It may be defined as the process of breaking the given text i.e. the character sequence into smaller units called tokens. The tokens may be the words, numbers or punctuation marks. It is also called word segmentation. Following is a simple example of tokenization −

Input − Mango, banana, pineapple and apple all are fruits.

Output −

Mango	Banana	Pineapple	and	Apple	all	are	Fruits

The process of breaking the given text can be done with the help of locating the word boundaries. The ending of a word and the beginning of a new word are called word boundaries. The writing system and the typographical structure of the words influence the boundaries.

In the Python NLTK module, we have different packages related to tokenization which we can use to divide the text into tokens as per our requirements. Some of the packages are as follows −

sent_tokenize package

As the name suggest, this package will divide the input text into sentences. We can import this package with the help of the following Python code −

```
from nltk.tokenize import sent_tokenize
```

word_tokenize package

This package divides the input text into words. We can import this package with the help of the following Python code −

```
from nltk.tokenize import word_tokenize
```

WordPunctTokenizer package

This package divides the input text into words as well as the punctuation marks. We can import this package with the help of the following Python code −

```
from nltk.tokenize import WordPuncttokenizer
```

Stemming

While working with words, we come across a lot of variations due to grammatical reasons. The concept of variations here means that we have to deal with different forms of the same words like *democracy, democratic,* and *democratization.* It is very necessary for machines to understand that these different words have the same base form. In this way, it would be useful to extract the base forms of the words while we are analyzing the text.

We can achieve this by stemming. In this way, we can say that stemming is the heuristic process of extracting the base forms of the words by chopping off the ends of words.

In the Python NLTK module, we have different packages related to stemming. These packages can be used to get the base forms of word. These packages use algorithms. Some of the packages are as follows −

PorterStemmer package

This Python package uses the Porter's algorithm to extract the base form. We can import this package with the help of the following Python code −

```
from nltk.stem.porter import PorterStemmer
```

For example, if we will give the word **'writing'** as the input to this stemmer them we will get the word **'write'** after stemming.

LancasterStemmer package

This Python package will use the Lancaster's algorithm to extract the base form. We can import this package with the help of the following Python code −

```
from nltk.stem.lancaster import LancasterStemmer
```

For example, if we will give the word **'writing'** as the input to this stemmer them we will get the word **'write'** after stemming.

SnowballStemmer package

This Python package will use the snowball's algorithm to extract the base form. We can import this package with the help of the following Python code −

```
from nltk.stem.snowball import SnowballStemmer
```

For example, if we will give the word **'writing'** as the input to this stemmer them we will get the word **'write'** after stemming.

All of these algorithms have different level of strictness. If we compare these three stemmers then the Porter stemmers is the least strict and Lancaster is the strictest.

Snowball stemmer is good to use in terms of speed as well as strictness.

Lemmatization

We can also extract the base form of words by lemmatization. It basically does this task with the use of a vocabulary and morphological analysis of words, normally aiming to remove inflectional endings only. This kind of base form of any word is called lemma.

The main difference between stemming and lemmatization is the use of vocabulary and morphological analysis of the words. Another difference is that stemming most commonly collapses derivationally related words whereas lemmatization commonly only collapses the different inflectional forms of a lemma. For example, if we provide the word saw as the input word then stemming might return the word 's' but lemmatization would attempt to return the word either see or saw depending on whether the use of the token was a verb or a noun.

In the Python NLTK module, we have the following package related to lemmatization process which we can use to get the base forms of word −

WordNetLemmatizer package

This Python package will extract the base form of the word depending upon whether it is used as a noun or as a verb. We can import this package with the help of the following Python code −

```
from nltk.stem import WordNetLemmatizer
```

Chunking: Dividing Data into Chunks

It is one of the important processes in natural language processing. The main job of chunking is to identify the parts of speech and short phrases like noun phrases. We have already studied the process of tokenization, the creation of tokens. Chunking basically is the labeling of those tokens. In other words, chunking will show us the structure of the sentence.

In the following section, we will learn about the different types of Chunking.

Types of chunking

There are two types of chunking. The types are as follows −

Chunking up

In this process of chunking, the object, things, etc. move towards being more general and the language gets more abstract. There are more chances of agreement. In this process, we zoom out. For example, if we will chunk up the question that "for what purpose cars are"? We may get the answer "transport".

Chunking down

In this process of chunking, the object, things, etc. move towards being more specific and the language gets more penetrated. The deeper structure would be examined in chunking down. In this process, we zoom in. For example, if we chunk down the question "Tell specifically about a car"? We will get smaller pieces of information about the car.

Example

In this example, we will do Noun-Phrase chunking, a category of chunking which will find the noun phrases chunks in the sentence, by using the NLTK module in Python −

Follow these steps in python for implementing noun phrase chunking −

Step 1 − In this step, we need to define the grammar for chunking. It would consist of the rules which we need to follow.

Step 2 − In this step, we need to create a chunk parser. It would parse the grammar and give the output.

Step 3 − In this last step, the output is produced in a tree format.

Let us import the necessary NLTK package as follows −

```
import nltk
```

Now, we need to define the sentence. Here, DT means the determinant, VBP means the verb, JJ means the adjective, IN means the preposition and NN means the noun.

```
sentence=[("a","DT"),("clever","JJ"),("fox","NN"),("was","VBP"),

("jumping","VBP"),("over","IN"),("the","DT"),("wall","NN")]
```

Now, we need to give the grammar. Here, we will give the grammar in the form of regular expression.

```
grammar = "NP:{<DT>?<JJ>*<NN>}"
```

We need to define a parser which will parse the grammar.

```
parser_chunking = nltk.RegexpParser(grammar)
```

The parser parses the sentence as follows −

```
parser_chunking.parse(sentence)
```

Next, we need to get the output. The output is generated in the simple variable called **output_chunk**.

```
Output_chunk = parser_chunking.parse(sentence)
```

Upon execution of the following code, we can draw our output in the form of a tree.

```
output.draw()
```

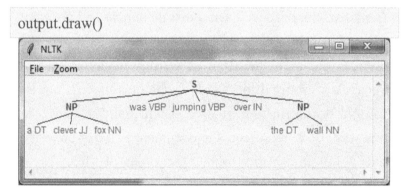

Bag of Word (BoW) Model

Bag of Word (BoW), a model in natural language processing, is basically used to extract the features from text so that the text can be used in modeling such that in machine learning algorithms.

Now the question arises that why we need to extract the features from text. It is because the machine learning algorithms cannot work with raw data and they need numeric data so that they can extract meaningful information out of it. The conversion of text data into numeric data is called feature extraction or feature encoding.

How it works

This is very simple approach for extracting the features from text. Suppose we have a text document and we want to convert it into numeric data or say want to extract the features out of it then first of all this model extracts a vocabulary from all the words in the document. Then by using a document term matrix, it will build a model. In this way, BoW represents the document as a bag of words only. Any information about the order or structure of words in the document is discarded.

Concept of document term matrix

The BoW algorithm builds a model by using the document term matrix. As the name suggests, the document term matrix is the matrix of various word counts that occur in the document. With the help of this matrix, the text document can be represented as a weighted combination of various words. By setting the threshold and choosing the words that are more meaningful, we can build a histogram of all the words in the documents that can be used as a feature vector. Following is an example to understand the concept of document term matrix −

Example

Suppose we have the following two sentences −

- **Sentence 1** − We are using the Bag of Words model.

- **Sentence 2** − Bag of Words model is used for extracting the features.

Now, by considering these two sentences, we have the following 13 distinct words −

- we
- are
- using
- the
- bag
- of
- words
- model
- is

- used
- for
- extracting
- features

Now, we need to build a histogram for each sentence by using the word count in each sentence –

- **Sentence 1** – [1,1,1,1,1,1,1,1,0,0,0,0,0]
- **Sentence 2** – [0,0,0,1,1,1,1,1,1,1,1,1,1]

In this way, we have the feature vectors that have been extracted. Each feature vector is 13-dimensional because we have 13 distinct words.

Concept of the Statistics:

The concept of the statistics is called TermFrequency-Inverse Document Frequency (tf-idf). Every word is important in the document. The statistics help us nderstand the importance of every word.

Term Frequency(tf)

It is the measure of how frequently each word appears in a document. It can be obtained by dividing the count of each word by the total number of words in a given document.

Inverse Document Frequency(idf)

It is the measure of how unique a word is to this document in the given set of documents. For calculating idf and formulating a distinctive feature vector, we need to reduce the weights of commonly occurring words like the and weigh up the rare words.

Building a Bag of Words Model in NLTK

In this section, we will define a collection of strings by using CountVectorizer to create vectors from these sentences.

Let us import the necessary package –

```
from           sklearn.feature_extraction.text           import
CountVectorizer
```

Now define the set of sentences.

```
Sentences = ['We are using the Bag of Word model', 'Bag
of Word model is

        used for extracting the features.']


vectorizer_count = CountVectorizer()
```

```
features_text                                        =
vectorizer.fit_transform(Sentences).todense()
```

print(vectorizer.vocabulary_)

The above program generates the output as shown below. It shows that we have 13 distinct words in the above two sentences −

{'we': 11, 'are': 0, 'using': 10, 'the': 8, 'bag': 1, 'of': 7, 'word': 12, 'model': 6, 'is': 5, 'used': 9, 'for': 4, 'extracting': 2, 'features': 3}

These are the feature vectors (text to numeric form) which can be used for machine learning.

Solving Problems

In this section, we will solve a few related problems.

Category Prediction:

In a set of documents, not only the words but the category of the words is also important; in which category of text a particular word falls. For example, we want to predict whether a given sentence belongs to the category email, news, sports, computer, etc. In the following example, we are going to use tf-idf to formulate a feature vector to find the category of documents. We will use the data from 20 newsgroup dataset of sklearn.

We need to import the necessary packages −

```
from sklearn.datasets import fetch_20newsgroups

from sklearn.naive_bayes import MultinomialNB

from          sklearn.feature_extraction.text          import
TfidfTransformer

from          sklearn.feature_extraction.text          import
CountVectorizer
```

Define the category map. We are using five different categories named Religion, Autos, Sports, Electronics and Space.

```
category_map                                              =
{'talk.religion.misc':'Religion','rec.autos"Autos',

  'rec.sport.hockey':'Hockey','sci.electronics':'Electronics',
'sci.space': 'Space'}
```

Create the training set −

```
training_data = fetch_20newsgroups(subset = 'train',

  categories = category_map.keys(), shuffle = True,
random_state = 5)
```

Build a count vectorizer and extract the term counts −

```
vectorizer_count = CountVectorizer()
```

```
train_tc                                                =
vectorizer_count.fit_transform(training_data.data)

print("\nDimensions of training data:", train_tc.shape)
```

The tf-idf transformer is created as follows −

```
tfidf = TfidfTransformer()

train_tfidf = tfidf.fit_transform(train_tc)
```

Now, define the test data −

```
input_data = [

   'Discovery was a space shuttle',

   'Hindu, Christian, Sikh all are religions',

   'We must have to drive safely',

   'Puck is a disk made of rubber',

   'Television, Microwave, Refrigrated all uses electricity'

]
```

The above data will help us train a Multinomial Naive Bayes classifier −

```
classifier            =            MultinomialNB().fit(train_tfidf,
training_data.target)
```

Transform the input data using the count vectorizer −

```
input_tc = vectorizer_count.transform(input_data)
```

Now, we will transform the vectorized data using the tfidf transformer −

```
input_tfidf = tfidf.transform(input_tc)
```

We will predict the output categories −

```
predictions = classifier.predict(input_tfidf)
```

The output is generated as follows −

```
for sent, category in zip(input_data, predictions):
    print('\nInput Data:', sent, '\n Category:', \
        category_map[training_data.target_names[category]])
```

The category predictor generates the following output −

Dimensions of training data: (2755, 39297)

Input Data: Discovery was a space shuttle
Category: Space

Input Data: Hindu, Christian, Sikh all are religions
Category: Religion

Input Data: We must have to drive safely
Category: Autos

Input Data: Puck is a disk made of rubber
Category: Hockey

Input Data: Television, Microwave, Refrigrated all uses electricity

Category: Electronics

Gender Finder

In this problem statement, a classifier would be trained to find the gender (male or female) by providing the names. We need to use a heuristic to construct a feature vector and train the classifier. We will be using the labeled data from the scikit-learn package. Following is the Python code to build a gender finder −

Let us import the necessary packages −

```
import random
```

```
from nltk import NaiveBayesClassifier

from nltk.classify import accuracy as nltk_accuracy

from nltk.corpus import names
```

Now we need to extract the last N letters from the input word. These letters will act as features −

```
def extract_features(word, N = 2):

  last_n_letters = word[-N:]

  return {'feature': last_n_letters.lower()}
```

```
if __name__=='__main__':
```

Create the training data using labeled names (male as well as female) available in NLTK −

```
male_list    =    [(name,    'male')    for    name    in
names.words('male.txt')]

female_list    =    [(name,    'female')    for    name    in
names.words('female.txt')]

data = (male_list + female_list)


random.seed(5)

random.shuffle(data)
```

Now, test data will be created as follows −

```
namesInput = ['Rajesh', 'Gaurav', 'Swati', 'Shubha']
```

Define the number of samples used for train and test with the following code

```
train_sample = int(0.8 * len(data))
```

Now, we need to iterate through different lengths so that the accuracy can be compared −

```
for i in range(1, 6):
```

```
print('\nNumber of end letters:', i)

features = [(extract_features(n, i), gender) for (n, gender)
in data]

train_data, test_data = features[:train_sample],

features[train_sample:]

classifier = NaiveBayesClassifier.train(train_data)
```

The accuracy of the classifier can be computed as follows
–

```
accuracy_classifier = round(100 * nltk_accuracy(classifier,
test_data), 2)

print('Accuracy = ' + str(accuracy_classifier) + '%')
```

Now, we can predict the output –

```
for name in namesInput:
    print(name,                                      '==>',
classifier.classify(extract_features(name, i)))
```

The above program will generate the following output –

```
Number of end letters: 1
Accuracy = 74.7%
Rajesh -> female
Gaurav -> male
Swati -> female
Shubha -> female

Number of end letters: 2
```

```
Accuracy = 78.79%
Rajesh -> male
Gaurav -> male
Swati -> female
Shubha -> female

Number of end letters: 3
Accuracy = 77.22%
Rajesh -> male
Gaurav -> female
Swati -> female
Shubha -> female

Number of end letters: 4
Accuracy = 69.98%
Rajesh -> female
Gaurav -> female
Swati -> female
Shubha -> female

Number of end letters: 5
Accuracy = 64.63%
Rajesh -> female
Gaurav -> female
Swati -> female
Shubha -> female
```

In the above output, we can see that accuracy in maximum number of end letters are two and it is decreasing as the number of end letters are increasing.

Topic Modeling: Identifying Patterns in Text Data:

We know that generally documents are grouped into topics. Sometimes we need to identify the patterns in a text that correspond to a particular topic. The technique of doing this is called topic modeling. In other words, we can say that topic modeling is a technique to uncover abstract themes or hidden structure in the given set of documents.

We can use the topic modeling technique in the following scenarios −

Text Classification

With the help of topic modeling, classification can be improved because it groups similar words together rather than using each word separately as a feature.

Recommender Systems

With the help of topic modeling, we can build the recommender systems by using similarity measures.

Algorithms for Topic Modeling

Topic modeling can be implemented by using algorithms. The algorithms are as follows −

Latent Dirichlet Allocation(LDA)

This algorithm is the most popular for topic modeling. It uses the probabilistic graphical models for implementing topic modeling. We need to import gensim package in Python for using LDA slgorithm.

Latent Semantic Analysis(LDA) or Latent Semantic Indexing(LSI)

This algorithm is based upon Linear Algebra. Basically it uses the concept of SVD (Singular Value Decomposition) on the document term matrix.

Non-Negative Matrix Factorization (NMF)

It is also based upon Linear Algebra.

All of the above mentioned algorithms for topic modeling would have the **number** of **topics** as a parameter, **Document-Word Matrix** as an input and **WTM (Word Topic Matrix)** & **TDM (Topic Document Matrix)** as output.

AI with Python – Analyzing Time Series Data

Predicting the next in a given input sequence is another important concept in machine learning. This chapter gives you a detailed explanation about analyzing time series data.

Introduction:

Time series data means the data that is in a series of particular time intervals. If we want to build sequence prediction in machine learning, then we have to deal with sequential data and time. Series data is an abstract of sequential data. Ordering of data is an important feature of sequential data.

Basic Concept of Sequence Analysis or Time Series Analysis

Sequence analysis or time series analysis is to predict the next in a given input sequence based on the previously observed. The prediction can be of anything that may come next: a symbol, a number, next day weather, next term in speech etc. Sequence analysis can be very handy in applications such as stock market analysis, weather forecasting, and product recommendations.

Example:

Consider the following example to understand sequence prediction. Here **A,B,C,D** are the given values and you have to predict the value **E** using a Sequence Prediction Model.

Installing Useful Packages

For time series data analysis using Python, we need to install the following packages –

Pandas

Pandas is an open source BSD-licensed library which provides high-performance, ease of data structure usage and data analysis tools for Python. You can install Pandas with the help of the following command –

```
pip install pandas
```

If you are using Anaconda and want to install by using the **conda** package manager, then you can use the following command –

```
conda install -c anaconda pandas
```

hmmlearn

It is an open source BSD-licensed library which consists of simple algorithms and models to learn Hidden Markov Models(HMM) in Python. You can install it with the help of the following command −

```
pip install hmmlearn
```

If you are using Anaconda and want to install by using the **conda** package manager, then you can use the following command −

```
conda install -c omnia hmmlearn
```

PyStruct

It is a structured learning and prediction library. Learning algorithms implemented in PyStruct have names such as conditional random fields(CRF), Maximum-Margin Markov Random Networks (M3N) or structural support vector machines. You can install it with the help of the following command −

```
pip install pystruct
```

CVXOPT

It is used for convex optimization based on Python programming language. It is also a free software package. You can install it with the help of following command −

```
pip install cvxopt
```

If you are using Anaconda and want to install by using the **conda** package manager, then you can use the following command −

```
conda install -c anaconda cvdoxt
```

Pandas: Handling, Slicing and Extracting Statistic from Time Series Data

Pandas is a very useful tool if you have to work with time series data. With the help of Pandas, you can perform the following −

- Create a range of dates by using the **pd.date_range**package

- Index pandas with dates by using the **pd.Series** package

- Perform re-sampling by using the **ts.resample** package

- Change the frequency

Example

The following example shows you handling and slicing the time series data by using Pandas. Note that here we are using the Monthly Arctic Oscillation data, which can be downloaded from <u>monthly.ao.index.b50.current.ascii</u> and can be converted to text format for our use.

Handling time series data

For handling time series data, you will have to perform the following steps −

The first step involves importing the following packages −

```
import numpy as np

import matplotlib.pyplot as plt

import pandas as pd
```

Next, define a function which will read the data from the input file, as shown in the code given below −

```
def read_data(input_file):

    input_data = np.loadtxt(input_file, delimiter = None)
```

Now, convert this data to time series. For this, create the range of dates of our time series. In this example, we keep one month as frequency of data. Our file is having the data which starts from January 1950.

```
dates     =     pd.date_range('1950-01',     periods     =
input_data.shape[0], freq = 'M')
```

In this step, we create the time series data with the help of Pandas Series, as shown below −

```
output = pd.Series(input_data[:, index], index = dates)
return output
```

```
if __name__ == '__main__':
```

Enter the path of the input file as shown here −

```
input_file = "/Users/admin/AO.txt"
```

Now, convert the column to timeseries format, as shown here −

```
timeseries = read_data(input_file)
```

Finally, plot and visualize the data, using the commands shown −

```
plt.figure()
timeseries.plot()
plt.show()
```

You will observe the plots as shown in the following images −

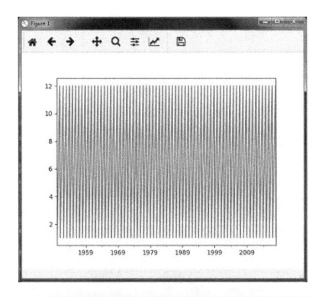

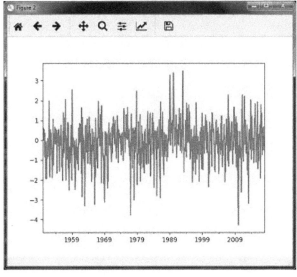

Slicing time series data

Slicing involves retrieving only some part of the time series data. As a part of the example, we are slicing the data only from 1980 to 1990. Observe the following code that performs this task −

```
timeseries['1980':'1990'].plot()

  <matplotlib.axes._subplots.AxesSubplot at 0xa0e4b00>


plt.show()
```

When you run the code for slicing the time series data, you can observe the following graph as shown in the image here −

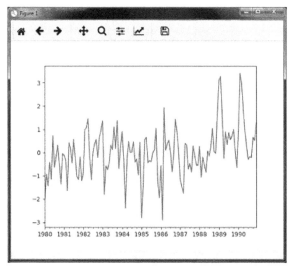

Extracting Statistic from Time Series Data:

You will have to extract some statistics from a given data, in cases where you need to draw some important conclusion. Mean, variance, correlation, maximum value, and minimum value are some of such statistics. You can use the following code if you want to extract such statistics from a given time series data −

Mean

You can use the **mean()** function, for finding the mean, as shown here −

```
timeseries.mean()
```

Then the output that you will observe for the example discussed is −

```
-0.11143128165238671
```

Maximum

You can use the **max()** function, for finding maximum, as shown here −

```
timeseries.max()
```

Then the output that you will observe for the example discussed is −

```
3.4952999999999999
```

Minimum

You can use the min() function, for finding minimum, as shown here −

```
timeseries.min()
```

Then the output that you will observe for the example discussed is −

```
-4.2656999999999998
```

Getting everything at once

If you want to calculate all statistics at a time, you can use the **describe()** function as shown here −

```
timeseries.describe()
```

Then the output that you will observe for the example discussed is −

```
count  817.000000
mean    -0.111431
std      1.003151
min     -4.265700
25%     -0.649430
50%     -0.042744
75%      0.475720
```

```
max        3.495300
dtype: float64
```

Re-sampling

You can resample the data to a different time frequency. The two parameters for performing re-sampling are −

- Time period
- Method

Re-sampling with mean()

You can use the following code to resample the data with the mean()method, which is the default method −

```
timeseries_mm = timeseries.resample("A").mean()

timeseries_mm.plot(style = 'g--')

plt.show()
```

Then, you can observe the following graph as the output of resampling using mean() −

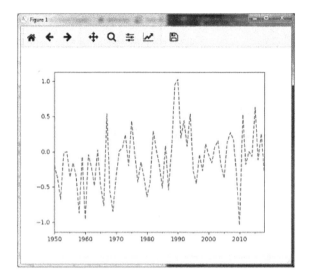

Re-sampling with median()

You can use the following code to resample the data using the **median()**method −

```
timeseries_mm = timeseries.resample("A").median()
timeseries_mm.plot()
plt.show()
```

Then, you can observe the following graph as the output of re-sampling with median() −

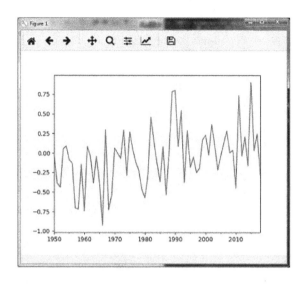

Rolling Mean

You can use the following code to calculate the rolling (moving) mean −

```
timeseries.rolling(window    =    12,    center    =
False).mean().plot(style = '-g')

plt.show()
```

Then, you can observe the following graph as the output of the rolling (moving) mean −

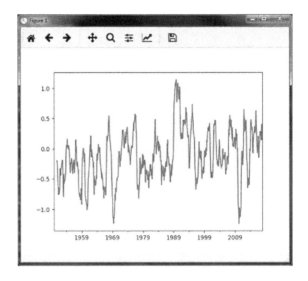

Analyzing Sequential Data by Hidden Markov Model (HMM):

HMM is a statistic model which is widely used for data having continuation and extensibility such as time series stock market analysis, health checkup, and speech recognition. This section deals in detail with analyzing sequential data using Hidden Markov Model (HMM).

Hidden Markov Model (HMM)

HMM is a stochastic model which is built upon the concept of Markov chain based on the assumption that probability of future stats depends only on the current process state rather any state that preceded it. For example, when tossing a coin, we cannot say that the result of the fifth toss will be a head. This is because a coin does not have any memory and the next result does not depend on the previous result.

Mathematically, HMM consists of the following variables –

States (S)

It is a set of hidden or latent states present in a HMM. It is denoted by S.

Output symbols (O)

It is a set of possible output symbols present in a HMM. It is denoted by O.

State Transition Probability Matrix (A)

It is the probability of making transition from one state to each of the other states. It is denoted by A.

Observation Emission Probability Matrix (B)

It is the probability of emitting/observing a symbol at a particular state. It is denoted by B.

Prior Probability Matrix (Π)

It is the probability of starting at a particular state from various states of the system. It is denoted by Π.

Hence, a HMM may be defined as $\lambda = (S,O,A,B,\pi)$,

where,

- $S = \{s_1,s_2,...,s_N\}$ is a set of N possible states,
- $O = \{o_1,o_2,...,o_M\}$ is a set of M possible observation symbols,
- A is an **NxN** state Transition Probability Matrix (TPM),
- B is an **NxM** observation or Emission Probability Matrix (EPM),
- π is an N dimensional initial state probability distribution vector.

Example: Analysis of Stock Market data

In this example, we are going to analyze the data of stock market, step by step, to get an idea about how the HMM works with sequential or time series data. Please note that we are implementing this example in Python.

Import the necessary packages as shown below −

```
import datetime

import warnings
```

Now, use the stock market data from the **matpotlib.finance**package, as shown here −

```
import numpy as np

from matplotlib import cm, pyplot as plt

from matplotlib.dates import YearLocator, MonthLocator

try:

    from            matplotlib.finance          import
quotes_historical_yahoo_och1

except ImportError:

    from matplotlib.finance import (

        quotes_historical_yahoo                          as
quotes_historical_yahoo_och1)



from hmmlearn.hmm import GaussianHMM
```

Load the data from a start date and end date, i.e., between two specific dates as shown here −

```
start_date = datetime.date(1995, 10, 10)

end_date = datetime.date(2015, 4, 25)
```

```
quotes = quotes_historical_yahoo_och1('INTC', start_date,
end_date)
```

In this step, we will extract the closing quotes every day.
For this, use the following command −

```
closing_quotes = np.array([quote[2] for quote in quotes])
```

Now, we will extract the volume of shares traded every
day. For this, use the following command −

```
volumes = np.array([quote[5] for quote in quotes])[1:]
```

Here, take the percentage difference of closing stock
prices, using the code shown below −

```
diff_percentages = 100.0 * np.diff(closing_quotes) /
closing_quotes[:-]

dates = np.array([quote[0] for quote in quotes], dtype =
np.int)[1:]

training_data = np.column_stack([diff_percentages,
volumes])
```

In this step, create and train the Gaussian HMM. For this,
use the following code −

```
hmm = GaussianHMM(n_components = 7,
covariance_type = 'diag', n_iter = 1000)

with warnings.catch_warnings():

    warnings.simplefilter('ignore')
```

```
hmm.fit(training_data)
```

Now, generate data using the HMM model, using the commands shown −

```
num_samples = 300
samples, _ = hmm.sample(num_samples)
```

Finally, in this step, we plot and visualize the difference percentage and volume of shares traded as output in the form of graph.

Use the following code to plot and visualize the difference percentages −

```
plt.figure()

plt.title('Difference percentages')

plt.plot(np.arange(num_samples), samples[:, 0], c = 'black')
```

Use the following code to plot and visualize the volume of shares traded −

```
plt.figure()

plt.title('Volume of shares')

plt.plot(np.arange(num_samples), samples[:, 1], c = 'black')

plt.ylim(ymin = 0)

plt.show()
```

AI with Python – Speech Recognition

In this chapter, we will learn about speech recognition using AI with Python.

Speech is the most basic means of adult human communication. The basic goal of speech processing is to provide an interaction between a human and a machine.

Speech processing system has mainly three tasks −

- **First**, speech recognition that allows the machine to catch the words, phrases and sentences we speak

- **Second**, natural language processing to allow the machine to understand what we speak, and

- **Third**, speech synthesis to allow the machine to speak.

This chapter focuses on **speech recognition**, the process of understanding the words that are spoken by human beings. Remember that the speech signals are captured with the help of a microphone and then it has to be understood by the system.

Building a Speech Recognizer

Speech Recognition or Automatic Speech Recognition (ASR) is the center of attention for AI projects like robotics. Without ASR, it is not possible to imagine a cognitive robot interacting with a human. However, it is not quite easy to build a speech recognizer.

Difficulties in developing a speech recognition system

Developing a high quality speech recognition system is really a difficult problem. The difficulty of speech recognition technology can be broadly characterized along a number of dimensions as discussed below –

- **Size of the vocabulary** – Size of the vocabulary impacts the ease of developing an ASR. Consider the following sizes of vocabulary for a better understanding.

  o A small size vocabulary consists of 2-100 words, for example, as in a voice-menu system

  o A medium size vocabulary consists of several 100s to 1,000s of words, for example, as in a database-retrieval task

  o A large size vocabulary consists of several 10,000s of words, as in a general dictation task.

  Note that, the larger the size of vocabulary, the harder it is to perform recognition.

- **Channel characteristics** – Channel quality is also an important dimension. For example, human speech contains high bandwidth with full frequency range, while a telephone speech consists of low bandwidth with limited frequency range. Note that it is harder in the latter.

- **Speaking mode** – Ease of developing an ASR also depends on the speaking mode, that is whether the speech is in isolated word mode, or connected word mode, or in a continuous speech mode. Note that a continuous speech is harder to recognize.

- **Speaking style** – A read speech may be in a formal style, or spontaneous and conversational with casual style. The latter is harder to recognize.

- **Speaker dependency** – Speech can be speaker dependent, speaker adaptive, or speaker independent. A speaker independent is the hardest to build.

- **Type of noise** – Noise is another factor to consider while developing an ASR. Signal to noise ratio may be in various ranges, depending on the acoustic environment that observes less versus more background noise –

  o If the signal to noise ratio is greater than 30dB, it is considered as high range o If the signal to noise ratio lies between 30dB to 10db, it is considered as medium SNR

o If the signal to noise ratio is lesser than 10dB, it is considered as low range

For example, the type of background noise such as stationary, non-human noise, background speech and crosstalk by other speakers also contributes to the difficulty of the problem.

- **Microphone characteristics** – The quality of microphone may be good, average, or below average. Also, the distance between mouth and micro-phone can vary. These factors also should be considered for recognition systems.

Despite these difficulties, researchers worked a lot on various aspects of speech such as understanding the speech signal, the speaker, and identifying the accents.

You will have to follow the steps given below to build a speech recognizer –

Visualizing Audio Signals - Reading from a File and Working on it

This is the first step in building speech recognition system as it gives an understanding of how an audio signal is structured. Some common steps that can be followed to work with audio signals are as follows –

Recording

When you have to read the audio signal from a file, then record it using a microphone, at first.

Sampling

When recording with microphone, the signals are stored in a digitized form. But to work upon it, the machine needs them in the discrete numeric form. Hence, we should perform sampling at a certain frequency and convert the signal into the discrete numerical form. Choosing the high frequency for sampling implies that when humans listen to the signal, they feel it as a continuous audio signal.

Example:

The following example shows a stepwise approach to analyze an audio signal, using Python, which is stored in a file. The frequency of this audio signal is 44,100 HZ.

Import the necessary packages as shown here −

```
import numpy as np

import matplotlib.pyplot as plt

from scipy.io import wavfile
```

Now, read the stored audio file. It will return two values: the sampling frequency and the audio signal. Provide the path of the audio file where it is stored, as shown here −

```
frequency_sampling,          audio_signal          =
wavfile.read("/Users/admin/audio_file.wav")
```

Display the parameters like sampling frequency of the audio signal, data type of signal and its duration, using the commands shown −

```
print('\nSignal shape:', audio_signal.shape)

print('Signal Datatype:', audio_signal.dtype)

print('Signal duration:', round(audio_signal.shape[0] /

float(frequency_sampling), 2), 'seconds')
```

This step involves normalizing the signal as shown below −

```
audio_signal = audio_signal / np.power(2, 15)
```

In this step, we are extracting the first 100 values from this signal to visualize. Use the following commands for this purpose −

```
audio_signal = audio_signal [:100]
time_axis  =  1000  *  np.arange(0,  len(signal),  1)  /
float(frequency_sampling)
```

Now, visualize the signal using the commands given below −

```
plt.plot(time_axis, signal, color='blue')

plt.xlabel('Time (milliseconds)')

plt.ylabel('Amplitude')

plt.title('Input audio signal')

plt.show()
```

You would be able to see an output graph and data extracted for the above audio signal as shown in the image here

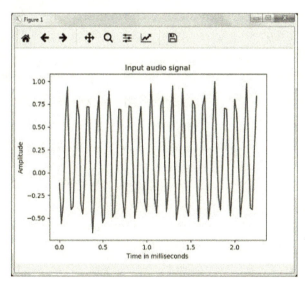

Signal shape: (132300,)

Signal Datatype: int16

Signal duration: 3.0 seconds

Characterizing the Audio Signal: Transforming to Frequency Domain:

Characterizing an audio signal involves converting the time domain signal into frequency domain, and understanding its frequency components, by. This is an important step because it gives a lot of information about the signal. You can use a mathematical tool like Fourier Transform to perform this transformation.

Example:

The following example shows, step-by-step, how to characterize the signal, using Python, which is stored in a file. Note that here we are using Fourier Transform mathematical tool to convert it into frequency domain.

Import the necessary packages, as shown here –

```
import numpy as np

import matplotlib.pyplot as plt

from scipy.io import wavfile
```

Now, read the stored audio file. It will return two values: the sampling frequency and the the audio signal. Provide the path of the audio file where it is stored as shown in the command here −

```
frequency_sampling,          audio_signal          =
wavfile.read("/Users/admin/sample.wav")
```

In this step, we will display the parameters like sampling frequency of the audio signal, data type of signal and its duration, using the commands given below −

```
print('\nSignal shape:', audio_signal.shape)

print('Signal Datatype:', audio_signal.dtype)

print('Signal duration:', round(audio_signal.shape[0] /

float(frequency_sampling), 2), 'seconds')
```

In this step, we need to normalize the signal, as shown in the following command −

```
audio_signal = audio_signal / np.power(2, 15)
```

This step involves extracting the length and half length of the signal. Use the following commands for this purpose −

```
length_signal = len(audio_signal)
half_length     =     np.ceil((length_signal     +     1)     /
2.0).astype(np.int)
```

Now, we need to apply mathematics tools for transforming into frequency domain. Here we are using the Fourier Transform.

```
signal_frequency = np.fft.fft(audio_signal)
```

Now, do the normalization of frequency domain signal and square it −

```
signal_frequency = abs(signal_frequency[0:half_length]) /
length_signal
```

```
signal_frequency **= 2
```

Next, extract the length and half length of the frequency transformed signal −

```
len_fts = len(signal_frequency)
```

Note that the Fourier transformed signal must be adjusted for even as well as odd case.

```
if length_signal % 2:
    signal_frequency[1:len_fts] *= 2
else:
    signal_frequency[1:len_fts-1] *= 2
```

Now, extract the power in decibal(dB) −

```
signal_power = 10 * np.log10(signal_frequency)
```

Adjust the frequency in kHz for X-axis −

```
x_axis = np.arange(0, len_half, 1) * (frequency_sampling / length_signal) / 1000.0
```

Now, visualize the characterization of signal as follows −

```
plt.figure()
plt.plot(x_axis, signal_power, color='black')
plt.xlabel('Frequency (kHz)')
plt.ylabel('Signal power (dB)')
plt.show()
```

You can observe the output graph of the above code as shown in the image below −

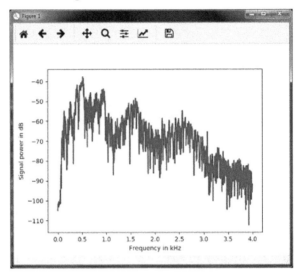

Generating Monotone Audio Signal:

The two steps that you have seen till now are important to learn about signals. Now, this step will be useful if you want to generate the audio signal with some predefined parameters. Note that this step will save the audio signal in an output file.

Example

In the following example, we are going to generate a monotone signal, using Python, which will be stored in a file. For this, you will have to take the following steps −

Import the necessary packages as shown −

```python
import numpy as np

import matplotlib.pyplot as plt

from scipy.io.wavfile import write
```

Provide the file where the output file should be saved

```python
output_file = 'audio_signal_generated.wav'
```

Now, specify the parameters of your choice, as shown −

```python
duration = 4 # in seconds

frequency_sampling = 44100 # in Hz

frequency_tone = 784

min_val = -4 * np.pi

max_val = 4 * np.pi
```

In this step, we can generate the audio signal, as shown −

```python
t = np.linspace(min_val, max_val, duration *
frequency_sampling)

audio_signal = np.sin(2 * np.pi * tone_freq * t)
```

Now, save the audio file in the output file −

```python
write(output_file, frequency_sampling, signal_scaled)
```

Extract the first 100 values for our graph, as shown −

```
audio_signal = audio_signal[:100]

time_axis  =  1000  *  np.arange(0,  len(signal),  1)  /
float(sampling_freq)
```

Now, visualize the generated audio signal as follows −

```
plt.plot(time_axis, signal, color='blue')

plt.xlabel('Time in milliseconds')

plt.ylabel('Amplitude')

plt.title('Generated audio signal')

plt.show()
```

You can observe the plot as shown in the figure given here −

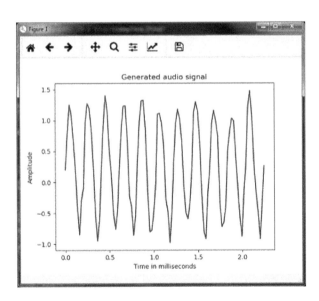

Feature Extraction from Speech:

This is the most important step in building a speech recognizer because after converting the speech signal into the frequency domain, we must convert it into the usable form of feature vector. We can use different feature extraction techniques like MFCC, PLP, PLP-RASTA etc. for this purpose.

Example

In the following example, we are going to extract the features from signal, step-by-step, using Python, by using MFCC technique.

Import the necessary packages, as shown here −

```
import numpy as np

import matplotlib.pyplot as plt

from scipy.io import wavfile

from python_speech_features import mfcc, logfbank
```

Now, read the stored audio file. It will return two values − the sampling frequency and the audio signal. Provide the path of the audio file where it is stored.

```
frequency_sampling,          audio_signal          =
wavfile.read("/Users/admin/audio_file.wav")
```

Note that here we are taking first 15000 samples for analysis.

```
audio_signal = audio_signal[:15000]
```

Use the MFCC techniques and execute the following command to extract the MFCC features −

```
features_mfcc = mfcc(audio_signal, frequency_sampling)
```

Now, print the MFCC parameters, as shown −

```
print('\nMFCC:\nNumber of windows =', features_mfcc.shape[0])
```

```
print('Length of each feature =', features_mfcc.shape[1])
```

Now, plot and visualize the MFCC features using the commands given below −

```
features_mfcc = features_mfcc.T
```

```
plt.matshow(features_mfcc)
```

```
plt.title('MFCC')
```

In this step, we work with the filter bank features as shown −

Extract the filter bank features −

```
filterbank_features = logfbank(audio_signal, frequency_sampling)
```

Now, print the filterbank parameters.

```
print('\nFilter bank:\nNumber of windows =',
filterbank_features.shape[0])

print('Length of each feature =',
filterbank_features.shape[1])
```

Now, plot and visualize the filterbank features.

```
filterbank_features = filterbank_features.T

plt.matshow(filterbank_features)

plt.title('Filter bank')

plt.show()
```

As a result of the steps above, you can observe the following outputs: Figure1 for MFCC and Figure2 for Filter Bank

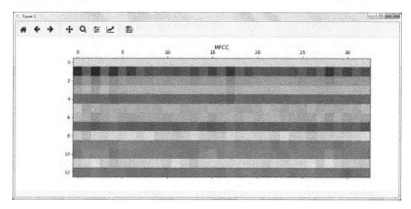

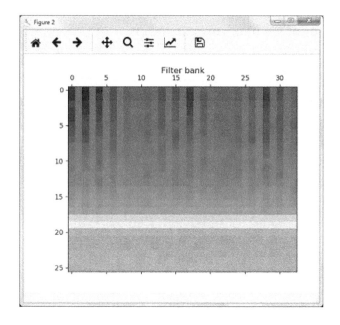

Recognition of Spoken Words:

Speech recognition means that when humans are speaking, a machine understands it. Here we are using Google Speech API in Python to make it happen. We need to install the following packages for this −

- **Pyaudio** − It can be installed by using **pip install Pyaudio** command.

- **SpeechRecognition** − This package can be installed by using **pip install SpeechRecognition.**

- **Google-Speech-API** – It can be installed by using the command **pip install google-api-python-client**.

Example:

Observe the following example to understand about recognition of spoken words –

Import the necessary packages as shown –

```
import speech_recognition as sr
```

Create an object as shown below –

```
recording = sr.Recognizer()
```

Now, the **Microphone()** module will take the voice as input –

```
with             sr.Microphone()            as           source:
recording.adjust_for_ambient_noise(source)

  print("Please Say something:")

  audio = recording.listen(source)
```

Now google API would recognize the voice and gives the output.

```
try:
   print("You          said:          \n"          +
recording.recognize_google(audio))
except Exception as e:
   print(e)
```

You can see the following output −

```
Please Say Something:
You said:
```

For example, if you said **google.com**, then the system recognizes it correctly as follows −

google.com

AI with Python – Heuristic Search

Heuristic search plays a key role in artificial intelligence. In this chapter, you will learn in detail about it.

Concept of Heuristic Search in AI:

Heuristic is a rule of thumb which leads us to the probable solution. Most problems in artificial intelligence are of exponential nature and have many possible solutions. You do not know exactly which solutions are correct and checking all the solutions would be very expensive.

Thus, the use of heuristic narrows down the search for solution and eliminates the wrong options. The method of using heuristic to lead the search in search space is called Heuristic Search. Heuristic techniques are very useful because the search can be boosted when you use them.

Difference between Uninformed and Informed Search

There are two types of control strategies or search techniques: uninformed and informed. They are explained in detail as given here −

Uninformed Search

It is also called blind search or blind control strategy. It is named so because there is information only about the problem definition, and no other extra information is available about the states. This kind of search techniques would search the whole state space for getting the solution. Breadth First Search (BFS) and Depth First Search (DFS) are the examples of uninformed search.

Informed Search

It is also called heuristic search or heuristic control strategy. It is named so because there is some extra information about the states. This extra information is useful to compute the preference among the child nodes to explore and expand. There would be a heuristic function associated with each node. Best First Search (BFS), A*, Mean and Analysis are the examples of informed search.

Constraint Satisfaction Problems (CSPs)

Constraint means restriction or limitation. In AI, constraint satisfaction problems are the problems which must be solved under some constraints. The focus must be on not to violate the constraint while solving such problems. Finally, when we reach the final solution, CSP must obey the restriction.

Real World Problem Solved by Constraint Satisfaction

The previous sections dealt with creating constraint satisfaction problems. Now, let us apply this to real world problems too. Some examples of real world problems solved by constraint satisfaction are as follows −

Solving algebraic relation

With the help of constraint satisfaction problem, we can solve algebraic relations. In this example, we will try to solve a simple algebraic relation **a*2 = b**. It will return the value of **a** and **b**within the range that we would define.

After completing this Python program, you would be able to understand the basics of solving problems with constraint satisfaction.

Note that before writing the program, we need to install Python package called python-constraint. You can install it with the help of the following command −

```
pip install python-constraint
```

The following steps show you a Python program for solving algebraic relation using constraint satisfaction −

Import the **constraint** package using the following command −

```
from constraint import *
```

Now, create an object of module named **problem()** as shown below −

```
problem = Problem()
```

Now, define variables. Note that here we have two variables a and b, and we are defining 10 as their range, which means we got the solution within first 10 numbers.

```
problem.addVariable('a', range(10))
```

```
problem.addVariable('b', range(10))
```

Next, define the particular constraint that we want to apply on this problem. Observe that here we are using the constraint **a*2 = b**.

```
problem.addConstraint(lambda a, b: a * 2 == b)
```

Now, create the object of **getSolution()** module using the following command −

```
solutions = problem.getSolutions()
```

Lastly, print the output using the following command −

```
print (solutions)
```

You can observe the output of the above program as follows −

```
[{'a': 4, 'b': 8}, {'a': 3, 'b': 6}, {'a': 2, 'b': 4}, {'a': 1, 'b': 2},
{'a': 0, 'b': 0}]
```

Magic Square

A magic square is an arrangement of distinct numbers, generally integers, in a square grid, where the numbers in each row , and in each column , and the numbers in the diagonal, all add up to the same number called the "magic constant".

The following is a stepwise execution of simple Python code for generating magic squares −

Define a function named **magic_square**, as shown below −

```
def magic_square(matrix_ms):
  iSize = len(matrix_ms[0])
  sum_list = []
```

The following code shows the code for vertical of squares −

```
for col in range(iSize):
  sum_list.append(sum(row[col] for row in matrix_ms))
```

The following code shows the code for horizantal of squares −

```
sum_list.extend([sum (lines) for lines in matrix_ms])
```

The following code shows the code for horizontal of squares −

```
dlResult = 0
for i in range(0,iSize):
   dlResult +=matrix_ms[i][i]
sum_list.append(dlResult)
drResult = 0
for i in range(iSize-1,-1,-1):
   drResult +=matrix_ms[i][i]
sum_list.append(drResult)

if len(set(sum_list))>1:
   return False
return True
```

Now, give the value of the matrix and check the output –

```
print(magic_square([[1,2,3], [4,5,6], [7,8,9]]))
```

You can observe that the output would be **False** as the sum is not up to the same number.

```
print(magic_square([[3,9,2], [3,5,7], [9,1,6]]))
```

You can observe that the output would be **True** as the sum is the same number, that is **15** here.

AI with Python – Gaming

Games are played with a strategy. Every player or team would make a strategy before starting the game and they have to change or build new strategy according to the current situation(s) in the game.

Search Algorithms

You will have to consider computer games also with the same strategy as above. Note that Search Algorithms are the ones that figure out the strategy in computer games.

How it works

The goal of search algorithms is to find the optimal set of moves so that they can reach at the final destination and win. These algorithms use the winning set of conditions, different for every game, to find the best moves.

Visualize a computer game as the tree. We know that tree has nodes. Starting from the root, we can come to the final winning node, but with optimal moves. That is the work of search algorithms. Every node in such tree represents a future state. The search algorithms search through this tree to make decisions at each step or node of the game.

Combinational Search

The major disadvantage of using search algorithms is that they are exhaustive in nature, which is why they explore the entire search space to find the solution that leads to wastage of resources. It would be more cumbersome if these algorithms need to search the whole search space for finding the final solution.

To eliminate such kind of problem, we can use combinational search which uses the heuristic to explore the search space and reduces its size by eliminating the possible wrong moves. Hence, such algorithms can save the resources. Some of the algorithms that use heuristic to search the space and save the resources are discussed here —

Minimax Algorithm

It is the strategy used by combinational search that uses heuristic to speed up the search strategy. The concept of Minimax strategy can be understood with the example of two player games, in which each player tries to predict the next move of the opponent and tries to minimize that function. Also, in order to win, the player always try to maximize its own function based on the current situation.

Heuristic plays an important role in such kind of strategies like Minimax. Every node of the tree would have a heuristic function associated with it. Based on that heuristic, it will take the decision to make a move towards the node that would benefit them the most.

Alpha-Beta Pruning

A major issue with Minimax algorithm is that it can explore those parts of the tree that are irrelevant, leads to the wastage of resources. Hence there must be a strategy to decide which part of the tree is relevant and which is irrelevant and leave the irrelevant part unexplored. Alpha-Beta pruning is one such kind of strategy.

The main goal of Alpha-Beta pruning algorithm is to avoid the searching those parts of the tree that do not have any solution. The main concept of Alpha-Beta pruning is to use two bounds named **Alpha**, the maximum lower bound, and **Beta**, the minimum upper bound. These two parameters are the values that restrict the set of possible solutions. It compares the value of the current node with the value of alpha and beta parameters, so that it can move to the part of the tree that has the solution and discard the rest.

Negamax Algorithm

This algorithm is not different from Minimax algorithm, but it has a more elegant implementation. The main disadvantage of using Minimax algorithm is that we need to define two different heuristic functions. The connection between these heuristic is that, the better a state of a game is for one player, the worse it is for the other player. In Negamax algorithm, the same work of two heuristic functions is done with the help of a single heuristic function.

Building Bots to Play Games

For building bots to play two player games in AI, we need to install the **easyAI** library. It is an artificial intelligence framework that provides all the functionality to build two-player games. You can download it with the help of the following command −

```
pip install easyAI
```

A Bot to Play Last Coin Standing

In this game, there would be a pile of coins. Each player has to take a number of coins from that pile. The goal of the game is to avoid taking the last coin in the pile. We will be using the class **LastCoinStanding** inherited from the **TwoPlayersGame** class of the **easyAI** library. The following code shows the Python code for this game −

Import the required packages as shown −

```
from easyAI import TwoPlayersGame, id_solve,
Human_Player, AI_Player

from easyAI.AI import TT
```

Now, inherit the class from the **TwoPlayerGame** class to handle all operations of the game –

```
class LastCoin_game(TwoPlayersGame):
  def __init__(self, players):
```

Now, define the players and the player who is going to start the game.

```
self.players = players
self.nplayer = 1
```

Now, define the number of coins in the game, here we are using 15 coins for the game.

```
self.num_coins = 15
```

Define the maximum number of coins a player can take in a move.

```
self.max_coins = 4
```

Now there are some certain things to define as shown in the following code. Define possible moves.

```
def possible_moves(self):

    return [str(a) for a in range(1, self.max_coins + 1)]
```

Define the removal of the coins

```
def make_move(self, move):

    self.num_coins -= int(move)
```

Define who took the last coin.

```
def win_game(self):

    return self.num_coins <= 0
```

Define when to stop the game, that is when somebody wins.

```
def is_over(self):

    return self.win()
```

Define how to compute the score.

```
def score(self):

    return 100 if self.win_game() else 0
```

Define number of coins remaining in the pile.

```
def show(self):
```

```
    print(self.num_coins, 'coins left in the pile')

if __name__ == "__main__":

    tt = TT()

    LastCoin_game.ttentry = lambda self: self.num_coins
```

Solving the game with the following code block –

```
r, d, m = id_solve(LastCoin_game,
    range(2, 20), win_score=100, tt=tt)
print(r, d, m)
```

Deciding who will start the game

```
game = LastCoin_game([AI_Player(tt), Human_Player()])
game.play()
```

You can find the following output and a simple play of this game –

```
d:2, a:0, m:1
d:3, a:0, m:1
d:4, a:0, m:1
d:5, a:0, m:1
d:6, a:100, m:4
1 6 4
15 coins left in the pile
Move #1: player 1 plays 4 :
11 coins left in the pile
```

```
Player 2 what do you play ? 2
Move #2: player 2 plays 2 :
9 coins left in the pile
Move #3: player 1 plays 3 :
6 coins left in the pile
Player 2 what do you play ? 1
Move #4: player 2 plays 1 :
5 coins left in the pile
Move #5: player 1 plays 4 :
1 coins left in the pile
Player 2 what do you play ? 1
Move #6: player 2 plays 1 :
0 coins left in the pile
```

A Bot to Play Tic Tac Toe

Tic-Tac-Toe is very familiar and one of the most popular games. Let us create this game by using the **easyAI** library in Python. The following code is the Python code of this game −

Import the packages as shown −

```
from easyAI import TwoPlayersGame, AI_Player,
Negamax

from easyAI.Player import Human_Player
```

Inherit the class from the **TwoPlayerGame** class to handle all operations of the game −

```
class TicTacToe_game(TwoPlayersGame):
```

```
def __init__(self, players):
```

Now, define the players and the player who is going to start the game −

```
self.players = players
self.nplayer = 1
```

Define the type of board −

```
self.board = [0] * 9
```

Now there are some certain things to define as follows −

Define possible moves

```
def possible_moves(self):
    return [x + 1 for x, y in enumerate(self.board) if y == 0]
```

Define the move of a player −

```
def make_move(self, move):
    self.board[int(move) - 1] = self.nplayer
```

To boost AI, define when a player makes a move –

```
def umake_move(self, move);
    self.board[int(move) - 1] = 0
```

Define the lose condition that an opponent have three in a line

```
def condition_for_lose(self):
    possible_combinations = [[1,2,3], [4,5,6], [7,8,9],
        [1,4,7], [2,5,8], [3,6,9], [1,5,9], [3,5,7]]
    return any([all([(self.board[z-1] == self.nopponent)
        for z in combination]) for combination in
    possible_combinations])
```

Define a check for the finish of game

```
def is_over(self):
    return    (self.possible_moves()    ==    []) or
    self.condition_for_lose()
```

Show the current position of the players in the game

```
def show(self):

    print('\n'+'\n'.join([' '.join([['.', 'O', 'X'][self.board[3*j + i]]

        for i in range(3)]) for j in range(3)]))
```

Compute the scores.

```
def scoring(self):

    return -100 if self.condition_for_lose() else 0
```

Define the main method to define the algorithm and start the game −

```
if __name__ == "__main__":

    algo = Negamax(7)

    TicTacToe_game([Human_Player(),
AI_Player(algo)]).play()
```

You can see the following output and a simple play of this game −

```
. . .
. . .
. . .
```

```
Player 1 what do you play ? 1
Move #1: player 1 plays 1 :
O . .
. . .

. . .
Move #2: player 2 plays 5 :
O . .
. X .
121
. . .
Player 1 what do you play ? 3
Move #3: player 1 plays 3 :
O . O
. X .

. . .
Move #4: player 2 plays 2 :
O X O
. X .

. . .
Player 1 what do you play ? 4
Move #5: player 1 plays 4 :
O X O
O X .

. . .
Move #6: player 2 plays 8 :
O X O
O X .
. X .
```

AI with Python – Neural Networks

Neural networks are parallel computing devices that are an attempt to make a computer model of brain. The main objective behind is to develop a system to perform various computational task faster than the traditional systems. These tasks include Pattern Recognition and Classification, Approximation, Optimization and Data Clustering.

What is Artificial Neural Networks (ANN)

Artificial Neural network (ANN) is an efficient computing system whose central theme is borrowed from the analogy of biological neural networks. ANNs are also named as Artificial Neural Systems, Parallel Distributed Processing Systems, and Connectionist Systems. ANN acquires large collection of units that are interconnected in some pattern to allow communications between them. These units, also referred to as **nodes** or **neurons**, are simple processors which operate in parallel.

Every neuron is connected with other neuron through a **connection link**. Each connection link is associated with a weight having the information about the input signal. This is the most useful information for neurons to solve a particular problem because the **weight** usually excites or inhibits the signal that is being communicated. Each neuron is having its internal state which is called **activation signal**. Output signals, which are produced after combining input signals and activation rule, may be sent to other units.

Installing Useful Packages

For creating neural networks in Python, we can use a powerful package for neural networks called **NeuroLab**. It is a library of basic neural networks algorithms with flexible network configurations and learning algorithms for Python. You can install this package with the help of the following command on command prompt −

```
pip install NeuroLab
```

If you are using the Anaconda environment, then use the following command to install NeuroLab −

```
conda install -c labfabulous neurolab
```

Building Neural Networks

In this section, let us build some neural networks in Python by using the NeuroLab package.

Following is a stepwise execution of the Python code for building a simple neural network perceptron based classifier –

Import the necessary packages as shown –

```
import matplotlib.pyplot as plt

import neurolab as nl
```

Enter the input values. Note that it is an example of supervised learning, hence you will have to provide target values too.

```
input = [[0, 0], [0, 1], [1, 0], [1, 1]]

target = [[0], [0], [0], [1]]
```

Create the network with 2 inputs and 1 neuron –

```
net = nl.net.newp([[0, 1],[0, 1]], 1)
```

Now, train the network. Here, we are using Delta rule for training.

```
error_progress = net.train(input, target, epochs=100, show=10, lr=0.1)
```

Now, visualize the output and plot the graph –

```
plt.figure()
```

```
plt.plot(error_progress)

plt.xlabel('Number of epochs')

plt.ylabel('Training error')

plt.grid()

plt.show()
```

You can see the following graph showing the training progress using the error metric −

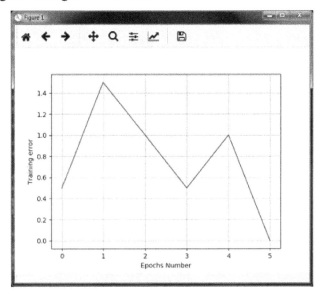

Single - Layer Neural Networks

In this example, we are creating a single layer neural network that consists of independent neurons acting on input data to produce the output. Note that we are using the text file named **neural_simple.txt** as our input.

Import the useful packages as shown −

```
import numpy as np

import matplotlib.pyplot as plt

import neurolab as nl
```

Load the dataset as follows −

```
input_data = np.loadtxt("/Users/admin/neural_simple.txt')
```

The following is the data we are going to use. Note that in this data, first two columns are the features and last two columns are the labels.

```
array([[2. , 4. , 0. , 0. ],

       [1.5, 3.9, 0. , 0. ],

       [2.2, 4.1, 0. , 0. ],

       [1.9, 4.7, 0. , 0. ],

       [5.4, 2.2, 0. , 1. ],

       [4.3, 7.1, 0. , 1. ],

       [5.8, 4.9, 0. , 1. ],

       [6.5, 3.2, 0. , 1. ],
```

```
[3. , 2. , 1. , 0. ],

[2.5, 0.5, 1. , 0. ],

[3.5, 2.1, 1. , 0. ],

[2.9, 0.3, 1. , 0. ],

[6.5, 8.3, 1. , 1. ],

[3.2, 6.2, 1. , 1. ],

[4.9, 7.8, 1. , 1. ],

[2.1, 4.8, 1. , 1. ]])
```

Now, separate these four columns into 2 data columns and 2 labels −

```
data = input_data[:, 0:2]

labels = input_data[:, 2:]
```

Plot the input data using the following commands −

```
plt.figure()
plt.scatter(data[:,0], data[:,1])
plt.xlabel('Dimension 1')
plt.ylabel('Dimension 2')
plt.title('Input data')
```

Now, define the minimum and maximum values for each dimension as shown here −

```
dim1_min, dim1_max = data[:,0].min(), data[:,0].max()
```

```
dim2_min, dim2_max = data[:,1].min(), data[:,1].max()
```

Next, define the number of neurons in the output layer as follows –

```
nn_output_layer = labels.shape[1]
```

Now, define a single-layer neural network –

```
dim1 = [dim1_min, dim1_max]

dim2 = [dim2_min, dim2_max]

neural_net = nl.net.newp([dim1, dim2], nn_output_layer)
```

Train the neural network with number of epochs and learning rate as shown –

```
error = neural_net.train(data, labels, epochs = 200, show =
20, lr = 0.01)
```

Now, visualize and plot the training progress using the following commands –

```
plt.figure()
plt.plot(error)
plt.xlabel('Number of epochs')
plt.ylabel('Training error')
plt.title('Training error progress')
plt.grid()
plt.show()
```

Now, use the test data-points in above classifier –

```
print('\nTest Results:')
```

```
data_test = [[1.5, 3.2], [3.6, 1.7], [3.6, 5.7],[1.6, 3.9]] for
item in data_test:
```

```
  print(item, '-->', neural_net.sim([item])[0])
```

You can find the test results as shown here −

[1.5, 3.2] --> [1. 0.]

[3.6, 1.7] --> [1. 0.]

[3.6, 5.7] --> [1. 1.]

[1.6, 3.9] --> [1. 0.]

You can see the following graphs as the output of the code discussed till now −

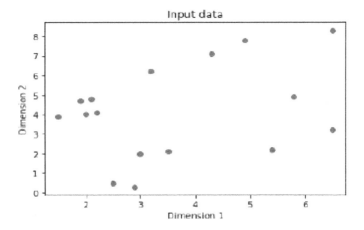

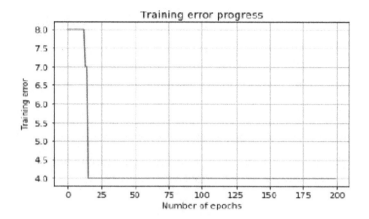

Multi-Layer Neural Networks

In this example, we are creating a multi-layer neural network that consists of more than one layer to extract the underlying patterns in the training data. This multilayer neural network will work like a regressor. We are going to generate some data points based on the equation: $y = 2x^2+8$.

Import the necessary packages as shown −

```
import numpy as np

import matplotlib.pyplot as plt

import neurolab as nl
```

Generate some data point based on the above mentioned equation −

```
min_val = -30
max_val = 30
num_points = 160
x = np.linspace(min_val, max_val, num_points)
y = 2 * np.square(x) + 8
y /= np.linalg.norm(y)
```

Now, reshape this data set as follows −

```
data = x.reshape(num_points, 1)
labels = y.reshape(num_points, 1)
```

Visualize and plot the input data set using the following commands −

```
plt.figure()
plt.scatter(data, labels)
plt.xlabel('Dimension 1')
plt.ylabel('Dimension 2')
plt.title('Data-points')
```

Now, build the neural network having two hidden layers with **neurolab** with **ten** neurons in the first hidden layer, **six** in the second hidden layer and **one** in the output layer.

```
neural_net = nl.net.newff([[min_val, max_val]], [10, 6, 1])
```

Now use the gradient training algorithm −

```
neural_net.trainf = nl.train.train_gd
```

Now train the network with goal of learning on the data generated above −

```
error = neural_net.train(data, labels, epochs = 1000, show = 100, goal = 0.01)
```

Now, run the neural networks on the training data-points −

```
output = neural_net.sim(data)

y_pred = output.reshape(num_points)
```

Now plot and visualization task −

```
plt.figure()

plt.plot(error)

plt.xlabel('Number of epochs')

plt.ylabel('Error')

plt.title('Training error progress')
```

Now we will be plotting the actual versus predicted output −

```
x_dense = np.linspace(min_val, max_val, num_points * 2)
y_dense_pred                                             =
neural_net.sim(x_dense.reshape(x_dense.size,1)).reshape(x
_dense.size)
plt.figure()
plt.plot(x_dense, y_dense_pred, '-', x, y, '.', x, y_pred, 'p')
plt.title('Actual vs predicted')
plt.show()
```

As a result of the above commands, you can observe the graphs as shown below −

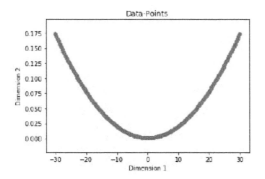

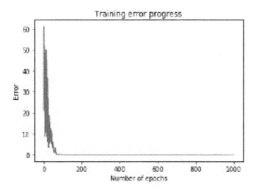

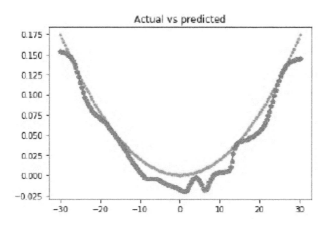

AI with Python – Reinforcement Learning

In this chapter, you will learn in detail about the concepts reinforcement learning in AI with Python.

Basics of Reinforcement Learning

This type of learning is used to reinforce or strengthen the network based on critic information. That is, a network being trained under reinforcement learning, receives some feedback from the environment. However, the feedback is evaluative and not instructive as in the case of supervised learning. Based on this feedback, the network performs the adjustments of the weights to obtain better critic information in future.

This learning process is similar to supervised learning but we might have very less information. The following figure gives the block diagram of reinforcement learning –

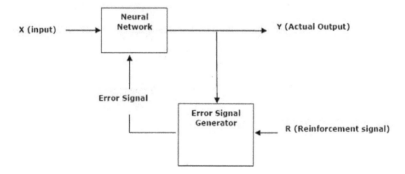

Building Blocks: Environment and Agent

Environment and Agent are main building blocks of reinforcement learning in AI. This section discusses them in detail –

Agent:

An agent is anything that can perceive its environment through sensors and acts upon that environment through effectors.

- A **human agent** has sensory organs such as eyes, ears, nose, tongue and skin parallel to the sensors, and other organs such as hands, legs, mouth, for effectors.

- A **robotic agent** replaces cameras and infrared range finders for the sensors, and various motors and actuators for effectors.

- A **software agent** has encoded bit strings as its programs and actions.

Agent Terminology:

The following terms are more frequently used in reinforcement learning in AI –

- **Performance Measure of Agent** – It is the criteria, which determines how successful an agent is.

- **Behavior of Agent** – It is the action that agent performs after any given sequence of percepts.

- **Percept** – It is agent's perceptual inputs at a given instance.

- **Percept Sequence** – It is the history of all that an agent has perceived till date.

- **Agent Function** – It is a map from the precept sequence to an action.

Environment:

Some programs operate in an entirely **artificial environment**confined to keyboard input, database, computer file systems and character output on a screen.

In contrast, some software agents, such as software robots or softbots, exist in rich and unlimited softbot domains. The simulator has a **very detailed**, and **complex environment**. The software agent needs to choose from a long array of actions in real time.

For example, a softbot designed to scan the online preferences of the customer and display interesting items to the customer works in the **real** as well as an **artificial** environment.

Properties of Environment:

The environment has multifold properties as discussed below −

- **Discrete/Continuous** − If there are a limited number of distinct, clearly defined, states of the environment, the environment is discrete , otherwise it is continuous. For example, chess is a discrete environment and driving is a continuous environment.

- **Observable/Partially Observable** − If it is possible to determine the complete state of the environment at each time point from the percepts, it is observable; otherwise it is only partially observable.

- **Static/Dynamic** − If the environment does not change while an agent is acting, then it is static; otherwise it is dynamic.

- **Single agent/Multiple agents** − The environment may contain other agents which may be of the same or different kind as that of the agent.

- **Accessible/Inaccessible** − If the agent's sensory apparatus can have access to the complete state of the environment, then the environment is accessible to that agent; otherwise it is inaccessible.

- **Deterministic/Non-deterministic** − If the next state of the environment is completely determined by the current state and the actions of the agent, then the environment is deterministic; otherwise it is non-deterministic.

- **Episodic/Non-episodic** − In an episodic environment, each episode consists of the agent perceiving and then acting. The quality of its action depends just on the episode itself. Subsequent episodes do not depend on the actions in the previous episodes. Episodic environments are much simpler because the agent does not need to think ahead.

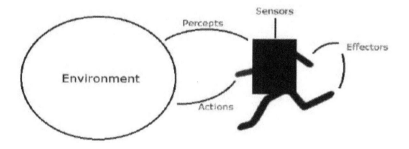

Constructing an Environment with Python

For building reinforcement learning agent, we will be using the **OpenAI Gym** package which can be installed with the help of the following command −

```
pip install gym
```

There are various environments in OpenAI gym which can be used for various purposes. Few of them are **Cartpole-v0, Hopper-v1**, and **MsPacman-v0**. They require different engines. The detail documentation of **OpenAI Gym** can be found on :

https://gym.openai.com/docs/#environments.

The following code shows an example of Python code for cartpole-v0 environment −

```
import gym
env = gym.make('CartPole-v0')
env.reset()
for _ in range(1000):
  env.render()
  env.step(env.action_space.sample())
```

You can construct other environments in a similar way.

Constructing a learning agent with Python:

For building reinforcement learning agent, we will be using the **OpenAI Gym** package as shown −

```python
import gym

env = gym.make('CartPole-v0')

for _ in range(20):

    observation = env.reset()

    for i in range(100):

        env.render()

        print(observation)

        action = env.action_space.sample()

        observation, reward, done, info = env.step(action)

        if done:

            print("Episode finished after {} timesteps".format(i+1))

            break
```

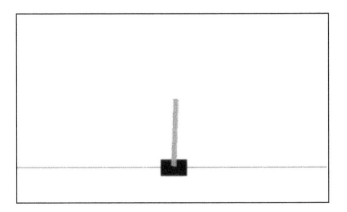

Observe that the cartpole can balance itself.

AI with Python – Genetic Algorithms

This chapter discusses Genetic Algorithms of AI in detail.

What are Genetic Algorithms?

Genetic Algorithms (GAs) are search based algorithms based on the concepts of natural selection and genetics. GAs are a subset of a much larger branch of computation known as Evolutionary Computation.

GAs were developed by John Holland and his students and colleagues at the University of Michigan, most notably David E. Goldberg. It has since been tried on various optimization problems with a high degree of success.

In GAs, we have a pool of possible solutions to the given problem. These solutions then undergo recombination and mutation (like in natural genetics), produces new children, and the process is repeated for various generations. Each individual (or candidate solution) is assigned a fitness value (based on its objective function value) and the fitter individuals are given a higher chance to mate and yield **fitter** individuals. This is in line with the Darwinian Theory of **Survival of the Fittest**.

Thus, it keeps **evolving** better individuals or solutions over generations, till it reaches a stopping criterion.

Genetic Algorithms are sufficiently randomized in nature, but they perform much better than random local search (where we just try random solutions, keeping track of the best so far), as they exploit historical information as well.

How to Use GA for Optimization Problems?

Optimization is an action of making design, situation, resource and system, as effective as possible. The following block diagram shows the optimization process −

Stages of GA mechanism for optimization process

The following is a sequence of steps of GA mechanism when used for optimization of problems.

- Step 1 − Generate the initial population randomly.

- Step 2 − Select the initial solution with best fitness values.

- Step 3 − Recombine the selected solutions using mutation and crossover operators.

- Step 4 − Insert an offspring into the population.

- Step 5 − Now, if the stop condition is met, return the solution with their best fitness value. Else go to step 2.

Installing Necessary Packages

For solving the problem by using Genetic Algorithms in Python, we are going to use a powerful package for GA called **DEAP**. It is a library of novel evolutionary computation framework for rapid prototyping and testing of ideas. We can install this package with the help of the following command on command prompt −

```
pip install deap
```

If you are using **anaconda** environment, then following command can be used to install deap −

```
conda install -c conda-forge deap
```

Implementing Solutions using Genetic Algorithms:

This section explains you the implementation of solutions using Genetic Algorithms.

Generating bit patterns

The following example shows you how to generate a bit string that would contain 15 ones, based on the **One Max** problem.

Import the necessary packages as shown −

```
import random
```

```
from deap import base, creator, tools
```

Define the evaluation function. It is the first step to create a genetic algorithm.

```
def eval_func(individual):

  target_sum = 15

  return len(individual) - abs(sum(individual) - target_sum),
```

Now, create the toolbox with the right parameters −

```
def create_toolbox(num_bits):

  creator.create("FitnessMax", base.Fitness, weights=(1.0,))

  creator.create("Individual", list, fitness=creator.FitnessMax)
```

Initialize the toolbox

```
  toolbox = base.Toolbox()

toolbox.register("attr_bool", random.randint, 0, 1)
```

```
toolbox.register("individual",              tools.initRepeat,
creator.Individual,

  toolbox.attr_bool, num_bits)

toolbox.register("population",      tools.initRepeat,      list,
toolbox.individual)
```

Register the evaluation operator −

```
toolbox.register("evaluate", eval_func)
```

Now, register the crossover operator −

```
toolbox.register("mate", tools.cxTwoPoint)
```

Register a mutation operator −

```
toolbox.register("mutate", tools.mutFlipBit, indpb = 0.05)
```

Define the operator for breeding −

```
toolbox.register("select", tools.selTournament, tournsize =
3)
return toolbox
```

```
if __name__ == "__main__":
    num_bits = 45
    toolbox = create_toolbox(num_bits)
    random.seed(7)
    population = toolbox.population(n = 500)
    probab_crossing, probab_mutating = 0.5, 0.2
    num_generations = 10
    print('\nEvolution process starts')
```

Evaluate the entire population −

```
fitnesses = list(map(toolbox.evaluate, population))
for ind, fit in zip(population, fitnesses):
    ind.fitness.values = fit
print('\nEvaluated', len(population), 'individuals')
```

Create and iterate through generations −

```
for g in range(num_generations):
    print("\n- Generation", g)
```

Selecting the next generation individuals −

```
offspring = toolbox.select(population, len(population))
```

Now, clone the selected individuals −

```
offspring = list(map(toolbox.clone, offspring))
```

Apply crossover and mutation on the offspring −

```
for child1, child2 in zip(offspring[::2], offspring[1::2]):

    if random.random() < probab_crossing:

    toolbox.mate(child1, child2)
```

Delete the fitness value of child

```
del child1.fitness.values

del child2.fitness.values
```

Now, apply mutation −

```
for mutant in offspring:
```

```
if random.random() < probab_mutating:

toolbox.mutate(mutant)

del mutant.fitness.values
```

Evaluate the individuals with an invalid fitness −

```
invalid_ind = [ind for ind in offspring if not
ind.fitness.valid]

fitnesses = map(toolbox.evaluate, invalid_ind)

for ind, fit in zip(invalid_ind, fitnesses):

    ind.fitness.values = fit

print('Evaluated', len(invalid_ind), 'individuals')
```

Now, replace population with next generation individual −

```
population[:] = offspring
```

Print the statistics for the current generations −

```
fits = [ind.fitness.values[0] for ind in population]
length = len(population)
```

```
mean = sum(fits) / length

sum2 = sum(x*x for x in fits)

std = abs(sum2 / length - mean**2)**0.5

print('Min =', min(fits), ', Max =', max(fits))

print('Average =', round(mean, 2), ', Standard deviation =',

round(std, 2))

print("\n- Evolution ends")
```

Print the final output −

```
  best_ind = tools.selBest(population, 1)[0]
  print('\nBest individual:\n', best_ind)
  print('\nNumber of ones:', sum(best_ind))
Following would be the output:
Evolution process starts
Evaluated 500 individuals
- Generation 0
Evaluated 295 individuals
Min = 32.0 , Max = 45.0
Average = 40.29 , Standard deviation = 2.61
- Generation 1
Evaluated 292 individuals
Min = 34.0 , Max = 45.0
Average = 42.35 , Standard deviation = 1.91
- Generation 2
Evaluated 277 individuals
Min = 37.0 , Max = 45.0
```

Average = 43.39 , Standard deviation = 1.46
... ...
- Generation 9
Evaluated 299 individuals
Min = 40.0 , Max = 45.0
Average = 44.12 , Standard deviation = 1.11
- Evolution ends
Best individual:
[0, 0, 0, 1, 0, 0, 0, 0, 0, 1, 0, 0, 0, 0, 1, 0, 1,
1, 0, 0, 0, 1, 0, 0, 0, 1, 1, 0, 0, 0, 1, 0, 0, 0,
1, 0, 0, 1, 1, 1, 0, 0, 1, 0, 1]
Number of ones: 15

Symbol Regression Problem:

It is one of the best known problems in genetic programming. All symbolic regression problems use an arbitrary data distribution, and try to fit the most accurate data with a symbolic formula. Usually, a measure like the RMSE (Root Mean Square Error) is used to measure an individual's fitness. It is a classic regressor problem and here we are using the equation $5x^3-6x^2+8x=1$. We need to follow all the steps as followed in the above example, but the main part would be to create the primitive sets because they are the building blocks for the individuals so the evaluation can start. Here we will be using the classic set of primitives.

The following Python code explains this in detail −

```
import operator
import math
import random
import numpy as np
from deap import algorithms, base, creator, tools, gp
def division_operator(numerator, denominator):
    if denominator == 0:
        return 1
    return numerator / denominator
def eval_func(individual, points):
    func = toolbox.compile(expr=individual)
    return math.fsum(mse) / len(points),
def create_toolbox():
    pset = gp.PrimitiveSet("MAIN", 1)
    pset.addPrimitive(operator.add, 2)
    pset.addPrimitive(operator.sub, 2)
    pset.addPrimitive(operator.mul, 2)
    pset.addPrimitive(division_operator, 2)
    pset.addPrimitive(operator.neg, 1)
    pset.addPrimitive(math.cos, 1)
    pset.addPrimitive(math.sin, 1)
    pset.addEphemeralConstant("rand101",          lambda:
random.randint(-1,1))
    pset.renameArguments(ARG0 = 'x')
    creator.create("FitnessMin", base.Fitness, weights = (-
1.0,))
```

```
creator.create("Individual",gp.PrimitiveTree,fitness=creator
.FitnessMin)
  toolbox = base.Toolbox()
  toolbox.register("expr", gp.genHalfAndHalf, pset=pset,
min_=1, max_=2)
  toolbox.expr)
  toolbox.register("population",tools.initRepeat,list,
toolbox.individual)
  toolbox.register("compile", gp.compile, pset = pset)
  toolbox.register("evaluate", eval_func, points = [x/10. for
x in range(-10,10)])
  toolbox.register("select", tools.selTournament, tournsize
= 3)
  toolbox.register("mate", gp.cxOnePoint)
  toolbox.register("expr_mut", gp.genFull, min_=0,
max_=2)
  toolbox.register("mutate", gp.mutUniform, expr =
toolbox.expr_mut, pset = pset)
  toolbox.decorate("mate", gp.staticLimit(key =
operator.attrgetter("height"), max_value = 17))
  toolbox.decorate("mutate", gp.staticLimit(key =
operator.attrgetter("height"), max_value = 17))
  return toolbox
if __name__ == "__main__":
  random.seed(7)
  toolbox = create_toolbox()
  population = toolbox.population(n = 450)
  hall_of_fame = tools.HallOfFame(1)
  stats_fit = tools.Statistics(lambda x: x.fitness.values)
  stats_size = tools.Statistics(len)
  mstats = tools.MultiStatistics(fitness=stats_fit, size =
stats_size)
  mstats.register("avg", np.mean)
```

```
mstats.register("std", np.std)
mstats.register("min", np.min)
mstats.register("max", np.max)
probab_crossover = 0.4
probab_mutate = 0.2
number_gen = 10
population,   log   =   algorithms.eaSimple(population,
toolbox,
   probab_crossover, probab_mutate, number_gen,
   stats = mstats, halloffame = hall_of_fame, verbose =
True)
```

Note that all the basic steps are same as used while generating bit patterns. This program will give us the output as min, max, std (standard deviation) after 10 number of generations.

AI with Python – Computer Vision

Computer vision is concerned with modeling and replicating human vision using computer software and hardware. In this chapter, you will learn in detail about this.

Computer Vision

Computer vision is a discipline that studies how to reconstruct, interrupt and understand a 3d scene from its 2d images, in terms of the properties of the structure present in the scene.

Computer Vision Hierarchy

Computer vision is divided into three basic categories as following −

- **Low-level vision** − It includes process image for feature extraction.

- **Intermediate-level vision** − It includes object recognition and 3D scene interpretation

- **High-level vision** − It includes conceptual description of a scene like activity, intention and behavior.

Computer Vision Vs Image Processing

Image processing studies image to image transformation. The input and output of image processing are both images.

Computer vision is the construction of explicit, meaningful descriptions of physical objects from their image. The output of computer vision is a description or an interpretation of structures in 3D scene.

Applications:

Computer vision finds applications in the following fields –

Robotics

- Localization-determine robot location automatically
- Navigation
- Obstacles avoidance
- Assembly (peg-in-hole, welding, painting)
- Manipulation (e.g. PUMA robot manipulator)
- Human Robot Interaction (HRI): Intelligent robotics to interact with and serve people

Medicine

- Classification and detection (e.g. lesion or cells classification and tumor detection)

- 2D/3D segmentation

- 3D human organ reconstruction (MRI or ultrasound)

- Vision-guided robotics surgery

Security

- Biometrics (iris, finger print, face recognition)

- Surveillance-detecting certain suspicious activities or behaviors

Transportation

- Autonomous vehicle

- Safety, e.g., driver vigilance monitoring

Industrial Automation Application

- Industrial inspection (defect detection)

- Assembly

- Barcode and package label reading

- Object sorting

- Document understanding (e.g. OCR)

Installing Useful Packages:

For Computer vision with Python, you can use a popular library called **OpenCV** (Open Source Computer Vision). It is a library of programming functions mainly aimed at the real-time computer vision. It is written in C++ and its primary interface is in C++. You can install this package with the help of the following command –

```
pip install opencv_python-X.X-cp36-cp36m-winX.whl
```

Here X represents the version of Python installed on your machine as well as the win32 or 64 bit you are having.

If you are using the **anaconda** environment, then use the following command to install OpenCV –

```
conda install -c conda-forge opencv
```

Reading, Writing and Displaying an Image:

Most of the CV applications need to get the images as input and produce the images as output. In this section, you will learn how to read and write image file with the help of functions provided by OpenCV.

OpenCV functions for Reading, Showing, Writing an Image File:

OpenCV provides the following functions for this purpose –

- **imread() function** – This is the function for reading an image. OpenCV imread() supports various image formats like PNG, JPEG, JPG, TIFF, etc.

- **imshow() function** – This is the function for showing an image in a window. The window automatically fits to the image size. OpenCV imshow() supports various image formats like PNG, JPEG, JPG, TIFF, etc.

- **imwrite() function** – This is the function for writing an image. OpenCV imwrite() supports various image formats like PNG, JPEG, JPG, TIFF, etc.

Example:

This example shows the Python code for reading an image in one format – showing it in a window and writing the same image in other format. Consider the steps shown below –

Import the OpenCV package as shown –

```
import cv2
```

Now, for reading a particular image, use the imread() function –

```
image = cv2.imread('image_flower.jpg')
```

For showing the image, use the **imshow()** function. The name of the window in which you can see the image would be **image_flower**.

```
cv2.imshow('image_flower',image)

cv2.destroyAllwindows()
```

Now, we can write the same image into the other format, say .png by using the imwrite() function –

```
cv2.imwrite('image_flower.png',image)
```

The output True means that the image has been successfully written as .png file also in the same folder.

```
True
```

Note − The function destroyallWindows() simply destroys all the windows we created.

Color Space Conversion:

In OpenCV, the images are not stored by using the conventional RGB color, rather they are stored in the reverse order i.e. in the BGR order. Hence the default color code while reading an image is BGR. The **cvtColor()** color conversion function in for converting the image from one color code to other.

Example

Consider this example to convert image from BGR to grayscale.

Import the **OpenCV** package as shown −

```
import cv2
```

Now, for reading a particular image, use the imread() function −

```
image = cv2.imread('image_flower.jpg')
```

Now, if we see this image using **imshow()** function, then we can see that this image is in BGR.

```
cv2.imshow('BGR_Penguins',image)
```

Now, use **cvtColor()** function to convert this image to grayscale.

```
image = cv2.cvtColor(image,cv2.COLOR_BGR2GRAY)

cv2.imshow('gray_penguins',image)
```

Edge Detection

Humans, after seeing a rough sketch, can easily recognize many object types and their poses. That is why edges play an important role in the life of humans as well as in the applications of computer vision. OpenCV provides very simple and useful function called **Canny()**for detecting the edges.

Example

The following example shows clear identification of the edges.

Import OpenCV package as shown −

```
import cv2

import numpy as np
```

Now, for reading a particular image, use the **imread()** function.

```
image = cv2.imread('Penguins.jpg')
```

Now, use the **Canny ()** function for detecting the edges of the already read image.

```
cv2.imwrite('edges_Penguins.jpg',cv2.Canny(image,200,300))
```

Now, for showing the image with edges, use the imshow() function.

```
cv2.imshow('edges', cv2.imread(''edges_Penguins.jpg'))
```

This Python program will create an image named **edges_penguins.jpg** with edge detection.

Face Detection

Face detection is one of the fascinating applications of computer vision which makes it more realistic as well as futuristic. OpenCV has a built-in facility to perform face detection. We are going to use the **Haar** cascade classifier for face detection.

Haar Cascade Data

We need data to use the Haar cascade classifier. You can find this data in our OpenCV package. After installing OpenCv, you can see the folder name **haarcascades**. There would be .xml files for different application. Now, copy all of them for different use and paste then in a new folder under the current project.

Example

The following is the Python code using Haar Cascade to detect the face of Small Baby shown in the following image −

Import the **OpenCV** package as shown −

```
import cv2

import numpy as np
```

Now, use the **HaarCascadeClassifier** for detecting face −

```
face_detection=

cv2.CascadeClassifier('D:/ProgramData/cascadeclassifier/

haarcascade_frontalface_default.xml')
```

Now, for reading a particular image, use the **imread()** function −

```
img = cv2.imread('baby.jpg')
```

Now, convert it into grayscale because it would accept gray images −

```
gray = cv2.cvtColor(img, cv2.COLOR_BGR2GRAY)
```

Now, using **face_detection.detectMultiScale**, perform actual face detection

```
faces = face_detection.detectMultiScale(gray, 1.3, 5)
```

Now, draw a rectangle around the whole face −

```
for (x,y,w,h) in faces:
    img = cv2.rectangle(img,(x,y),(x+w, y+h),(255,0,0),3)
cv2.imwrite('Face_baby.jpg',img)
```

This Python program will create an image named **Face_baby.jpg** with face detection as shown

Eye Detection

Eye detection is another fascinating application of computer vision which makes it more realistic as well as futuristic. OpenCV has a built-in facility to perform eye detection. We are going to use the **Haar cascade** classifier for eye detection.

Example:

The following example gives the Python code using Haar Cascade to detect the face of Amitabh Bachan given in the following image –

Import OpenCV package as shown −

import cv2

import numpy as np

Now, use the **HaarCascadeClassifier** for detecting face −

eye_cascade   =
cv2.CascadeClassifier('D:/ProgramData/cascadeclassifier/h
aarcascade_eye.xml')

Now, for reading a particular image, use the **imread()** function

img = cv2.imread('AB_Eye.jpg')

Now, convert it into grayscale because it would accept grey images −

gray = cv2.cvtColor(img, cv2.COLOR_BGR2GRAY)

Now with the help of **eye_cascade.detectMultiScale**, perform actual face detection

```
eyes = eye_cascade.detectMultiScale(gray, 1.03, 5)
```

Now, draw a rectangle around the whole face −

```
for (ex,ey,ew,eh) in eyes:
    img         =         cv2.rectangle(img,(ex,ey),(ex+ew,
ey+eh),(0,255,0),2)

cv2.imwrite('Eye_AB.jpg',img)
```

This Python program will create an image named **Eye_AB.jpg**with eye detection as shown −

AI with Python – Deep Learning

Artificial Neural Network (ANN) it is an efficient computing system, whose central theme is borrowed from the analogy of biological neural networks. Neural networks are one type of model for machine learning. In the mid-1980s and early 1990s, much important architectural advancements were made in neural networks. In this chapter, you will learn more about Deep Learning, an approach of AI.

Deep learning emerged from a decade's explosive computational growth as a serious contender in the field. Thus, deep learning is a particular kind of machine learning whose algorithms are inspired by the structure and function of human brain.

Machine Learning v/s Deep Learning

Deep learning is the most powerful machine learning technique these days. It is so powerful because they learn the best way to represent the problem while learning how to solve the problem. A comparison of Deep learning and Machine learning is given below −

Data Dependency

The first point of difference is based upon the performance of DL and ML when the scale of data increases. When the data is large, deep learning algorithms perform very well.

Machine Dependency

Deep learning algorithms need high-end machines to work perfectly. On the other hand, machine learning algorithms can work on low-end machines too.

Feature Extraction

Deep learning algorithms can extract high level features and try to learn from the same too. On the other hand, an expert is required to identify most of the features extracted by machine learning.

Time of Execution

Execution time depends upon the numerous parameters used in an algorithm. Deep learning has more parameters than machine learning algorithms. Hence, the execution time of DL algorithms, specially the training time, is much more than ML algorithms. But the testing time of DL algorithms is less than ML algorithms.

Approach to Problem Solving

Deep learning solves the problem end-to-end while machine learning uses the traditional way of solving the problem i.e. by breaking down it into parts.

Convolutional Neural Network (CNN)

Convolutional neural networks are the same as ordinary neural networks because they are also made up of neurons that have learnable weights and biases. Ordinary neural networks ignore the structure of input data and all the data is converted into 1-D array before feeding it into the network. This process suits the regular data, however if the data contains images, the process may be cumbersome.

CNN solves this problem easily. It takes the 2D structure of the images into account when they process them, which allows them to extract the properties specific to images. In this way, the main goal of CNNs is to go from the raw image data in the input layer to the correct class in the output layer. The only difference between an ordinary NNs and CNNs is in the treatment of input data and in the type of layers.

Architecture Overview of CNNs

Architecturally, the ordinary neural networks receive an input and transform it through a series of hidden layer. Every layer is connected to the other layer with the help of neurons. The main disadvantage of ordinary neural networks is that they do not scale well to full images.

The architecture of CNNs have neurons arranged in 3 dimensions called width, height and depth. Each neuron in the current layer is connected to a small patch of the output from the previous layer. It is similar to overlaying a $N \times N$ filter on the input image. It uses **M** filters to be sure about getting all the details. These **M**filters are feature extractors which extract features like edges, corners, etc.

Layers used to construct CNNs

Following layers are used to construct CNNs –

- **Input Layer** – It takes the raw image data as it is.

- **Convolutional Layer** – This layer is the core building block of CNNs that does most of the computations. This layer computes the convolutions between the neurons and the various patches in the input.

- **Rectified Linear Unit Layer** – It applies an activation function to the output of the previous layer. It adds non-linearity to the network so that it can generalize well to any type of function.

- **Pooling Layer** – Pooling helps us to keep only the important parts as we progress in the network. Pooling layer operates independently on every depth slice of the input and resizes it spatially. It uses the MAX function.

- **Fully Connected layer/Output layer** – This layer computes the output scores in the last layer. The resulting output is of the size $1 \times 1 \times L$, where L is the number training dataset classes.

Installing Useful Python Packages

You can use **Keras**, which is an high level neural networks API, written in Python and capable of running on top of TensorFlow, CNTK or Theno. It is compatible with Python 2.7-3.6. You can learn more about it from https://keras.io/.

Use the following commands to install keras –

```
pip install keras
```

On **conda** environment, you can use the following command –

```
conda install –c conda-forge keras
```

Building Linear Regressor using ANN

In this section, you will learn how to build a linear regressor using artificial neural networks. You can use **KerasRegressor** to achieve this. In this example, we are using the Boston house price dataset with 13 numerical for properties in Boston. The Python code for the same is shown here –

Import all the required packages as shown −

```
import numpy

import pandas

from keras.models import Sequential

from keras.layers import Dense

from keras.wrappers.scikit_learn import KerasRegressor

from sklearn.model_selection import cross_val_score

from sklearn.model_selection import KFold
```

Now, load our dataset which is saved in local directory.

```
dataframe = pandas.read_csv("/Usrrs/admin/data.csv",
delim_whitespace = True, header = None)

dataset = dataframe.values
```

Now, divide the data into input and output variables i.e. X and Y −

```
X = dataset[:,0:13]

Y = dataset[:,13]
```

Since we use baseline neural networks, define the model −

```
def baseline_model():
```

Now, create the model as follows −

```
model_regressor = Sequential()
model_regressor.add(Dense(13,     input_dim     =     13,
kernel_initializer = 'normal',

  activation = 'relu'))
model_regressor.add(Dense(1,     kernel_initializer     =
'normal'))
```

Next, compile the model −

```
model_regressor.compile(loss='mean_squared_error',
optimizer='adam')

return model_regressor
```

Now, fix the random seed for reproducibility as follows −

```
seed = 7

numpy.random.seed(seed)
```

The Keras wrapper object for use in **scikit-learn** as a regression estimator is called **KerasRegressor**. In this section, we shall evaluate this model with standardize data set.

```
estimator = KerasRegressor(build_fn = baseline_model,
nb_epoch = 100, batch_size = 5, verbose = 0)
```

```
kfold = KFold(n_splits = 10, random_state = seed)

baseline_result = cross_val_score(estimator, X, Y, cv = kfold)

print("Baseline:     %.2f     (%.2f)     MSE"     % (Baseline_result.mean(),Baseline_result.std()))
```

The output of the code shown above would be the estimate of the model's performance on the problem for unseen data. It will be the mean squared error, including the average and standard deviation across all 10 folds of the cross validation evaluation.

Image Classifier: An Application of Deep Learning

Convolutional Neural Networks (CNNs) solve an image classification problem, that is to which class the input image belongs to. You can use Keras deep learning library. Note that we are using the training and testing data set of images of cats and dogs from following link https://www.kaggle.com/c/dogs-vs-cats/data.

Import the important keras libraries and packages as shown −

The following package called sequential will initialize the neural networks as sequential network.

```
from keras.models import Sequential
```

The following package called **Conv2D** is used to perform the convolution operation, the first step of CNN.

```
from keras.layers import Conv2D
```

The following package called **MaxPoling2D** is used to perform the pooling operation, the second step of CNN.

```
from keras.layers import MaxPooling2D
```

The following package called **Flatten** is the process of converting all the resultant 2D arrays into a single long continuous linear vector.

```
from keras.layers import Flatten
```

The following package called **Dense** is used to perform the full connection of the neural network, the fourth step of CNN.

```
from keras.layers import Dense
```

Now, create an object of the sequential class.

```
S_classifier = Sequential()
```

Now, next step is coding the convolution part.

```
S_classifier.add(Conv2D(32, (3, 3), input_shape = (64, 64, 3), activation = 'relu'))
```

Here **relu** is the rectifier function.

Now, the next step of CNN is the pooling operation on the resultant feature maps after convolution part.

```
S-classifier.add(MaxPooling2D(pool_size = (2, 2)))
```

Now, convert all the pooled images into a continuous vector by using flattering –

```
S_classifier.add(Flatten())
```

Next, create a fully connected layer.

```
S_classifier.add(Dense(units = 128, activation = 'relu'))
```

Here, 128 is the number of hidden units. It is a common practice to define the number of hidden units as the power of 2.

Now, initialize the output layer as follows –

```
S_classifier.add(Dense(units = 1, activation = 'sigmoid'))
```

Now, compile the CNN, we have built –

```
S_classifier.compile(optimizer = 'adam', loss = 'binary_crossentropy', metrics = ['accuracy'])
```

Here optimizer parameter is to choose the stochastic gradient descent algorithm, loss parameter is to choose the loss function and metrics parameter is to choose the performance metric.

Now, perform image augmentations and then fit the images to the neural networks −

```
train_datagen    =    ImageDataGenerator(rescale    =
1./255,shear_range = 0.2,

zoom_range = 0.2,

horizontal_flip = True)

test_datagen = ImageDataGenerator(rescale = 1./255)


training_set =

train_datagen.flow_from_directory("/Users/admin/training
_set",target_size =

    (64, 64),batch_size = 32,class_mode = 'binary')


test_set =

  test_datagen.flow_from_directory('test_set',target_size =

    (64, 64),batch_size = 32,class_mode = 'binary')
```

Now, fit the data to the model we have created −

```
classifier.fit_generator(training_set,steps_per_epoch    =
8000,epochs =

25,validation_data = test_set,validation_steps = 2000)
```

Here steps_per_epoch have the number of training images.

Now as the model has been trained, we can use it for prediction as follows −

```
from keras.preprocessing import image


test_image                                              =
image.load_img('dataset/single_prediction/cat_or_dog_1.jp
g',

target_size = (64, 64))


test_image = image.img_to_array(test_image)


test_image = np.expand_dims(test_image, axis = 0)


result = classifier.predict(test_image)
```

```
training_set.class_indices

if result[0][0] == 1:
prediction = 'dog'

else:
    prediction = 'cat'
```

Thank You!

www.ingramcontent.com/pod-product-compliance
Lightning Source LLC
Chambersburg PA
CBHW031217050326
40689CB00009B/1371